Rudo Ensayo

Rudo Ensayo

A DESCRIPTION OF
SONORA AND ARIZONA
IN 1764

Juan Nentvig, S.J.

Translated, Clarified, and Annotated by
ALBERTO FRANCISCO PRADEAU AND
ROBERT R. RASMUSSEN

UNIVERSITY OF ARIZONA PRESS
Tucson, Arizona

About the Translators . . .

Dr. Alberto Pradeau's interest in the territory ceded to the United States by the treaty of Guadalupe Hidalgo February 2, 1848, began in 1908 with the reading of Samuel Woodworth Cozzens' book *The Ancient Cibola: The Marvellous Country*. Since 1940 this interest has been a relentlessly pursued hobby, and the present version of *Rudo Ensayo* is the result of personal knowledge, firsthand experience, and extensive research. Dr. Pradeau is a dental surgeon born in Sonora, Mexico, where he received his early education, and is a graduate of the University of Southern California.

Robert R. Rasmussen earned a bachelor's degree and a master's degree from California State University at Los Angeles in English literature. Having read the life of Father Eusebio Kino and become interested in the Catholic experience in New Spain during the seventeenth and eighteenth centuries, he worked very closely with Dr. Pradeau for several years in the preparation of this volume.

The University of Arizona Press
www.uapress.arizona.edu

Century Collection edition 2017

Printed in the United States of America
22 21 20 19 18 17 7 6 5 4 3 2

ISBN-13: 978-0-8165-0696-5 (cloth)
ISBN-13: 978-0-8165-0624-8 (paper)
ISBN-13: 978-0-8165-3578-1 (Century Collection paper)

Library of Congress Cataloging-in-Publication Data
Nentvig, Juan, 1713–1768.
Rudo ensayo: a description of Sonora and Arizona in 1764.
Translation of the copy of the author's ms. in the Archivo General de la Nación, Mexico City, History Section, v. 393 which has title: Descripción geográfica, natural y curiosa de la Provincia de Sonora por un amigo de el servicio de Dios y de el Rey Nuestro Señor; commonly known as Rudo ensayo.
Bibliography: p.
Includes indexes.
1. Sonora, Mexico—Description and travel. 2. Indians of Mexico—Sonora. 3. Jesuits—Mexico—Sonora. 4. Arizona—Description and Travel. 5. Indians of North America—Arizona. 6. Jesuits—Arizona. I. Pradeau Avilés, Alberto Francisco, 1894– II. Rasmussen, Robert R. III. Title.
F1346.N413 1979 972'.1 79-20420
ISBN 0-8165-0696-5
ISBN 0-8165-0624-8 pbk.

♾ This paper meets the requirements of ANSI/NISO Z39.48-1992 (Permanence of Paper).

Gratefully Dedicated to
Father Ernest J. Burrus, S.J., and Harmon J. Middaugh

Contents

Preface

Studying the history of southern Arizona and Sonora is a fascinating activity, as is trying to understand the eighteenth-century mind. *Rudo Ensayo* offers a unique blend of both. The work may be read to gain knowledge of the history of the region, the quest for metals, fauna and flora, and missionary work among the Indians, to mention just a few subjects. But even more than these, the work offers an interesting view of eighteenth-century thinking. Father Juan Nentvig's manuscript was written in a century of exploration when people were willing to believe that far-off lands were filled with incredible mysteries; it is crammed with information interlaced with colorful but impossible tales.

Nentvig writes of a double-headed eagle with a casual matter-of-factness. He speaks of the spasm herb that relieves tension in man or beast, and describes how animals recuperate immediately following its administration. He writes of jojoba nuts, their power to treat arrow wounds, and includes a personal testimonial, describing how he was cured instantly of a sharp pain in his rib cage. He tells of a palm frond that can make barren women fertile and fumes of a cocoon that will cure malaria.

Furthermore, one is astounded by his account of a tarantula biting off the hoof of a horse as the animal gallops by, and a description of a rock with a liquid center. There is an amazing story of the curative powers of the roots of the jaramatraca tree. Declaring himself an eyewitness, Nentvig discloses that a cowboy was restored to health overnight after being trampled by a horse. His face mangled with bones exposed, he received treatment consisting of a poultice made from this wondrous plant and was healed by the next day. Just as astonishing, Nentvig refers to a mining site so rich in silver that rocks found there will flatten when struck with a hammer. And he tells of an old man who discovered a vein of silver so rich he merely had to cut off the amount he wanted with a knife.

Then, too, Father Nentvig takes us on an imaginary flight over the province of Sonora, pointing out the mission stations, the mining towns, reales de minas, Indian villages, and Spanish settlements of the 1760s. His geographical description is amazingly accurate, and his close attention to detail sets the work above other writings covering the period and area. His is the best of the eighteenth-century histories of Sonora and southern Arizona—an account by a learned European who had a keen sense of responsibility and was capable of judging rather impartially, describing life in Sonora thoroughly and systematically.

We also follow Father Nentvig's frustrations as he tries to force a European lifestyle on the Pimas, Seris, and the Opatas, whom he praises as the best Christians and most loyal allies, and on the wily Apaches, whom he condemns as the most hostile and uncontrollable enemy. He rebukes the Indians for their failure to follow the ways of the Spaniard and is awed by the natives' ability to survive and excel in the tortuous desert and rugged mountains.

Nentvig quotes an old-time Sonoran missionary as saying that "there are no Christians in the world who recite the catechism more often and know it less than these Indians." Nentvig points with pride at a group of natives that insists upon hearing mass more often than required, and he fails to realize that these natives come primarily to be fed and only tolerate the spiritual enlightenment as the price they have to pay for the priest's gift of food.

Dealing in some detail with the customs of the Indians, Nentvig offers insights into tribal life. He admires the patience of Indian women who wouldn't accept modern weaving methods and continued using their slow way, which he describes minutely, with extraordinary results. The image here is of an independent people who long to live in the old ways and survive with the ancient traditions. The idealistic German priest refers to them as his "spiritual children" and encourages them to till the soil and live more industriously.

Almost killed in an Indian rebellion only a year after he arrived in

Sonora, Nentvig survived a siege in a small mission church and struggled onward in keeping with the tenets of his faith—opposing the Indians where he had to, supporting them against the government when necessary, and always spreading the word of God wherever he went. His chapters dealing with the Indians are among the finest ever written.

Present-day scholars are indebted both to a Franciscan friar, probably Manuel de la Vega, who was commissary general for the Indies in 1770, for gathering a number of manuscripts, and to an illustrious viceroy of New Spain, Juan Vicente Güemes-Pacheco y Padilla, who on February 21, 1790, decreed the collection of all manuscripts pertaining to New Spain and appointed another Franciscan friar, Francisco García Figueroa, a prominent member of his order, to accomplish the task. In less than three years García Figueroa amassed 32 volumes, over 1,000 folios, of precious documents. In the Franciscan archives among the de la Vega papers the *Descripción de Sonora* was found.

As for the title *Rudo Ensayo,* meaning rough essay, it was not literally part of the original manuscript but was applied by Buckingham Smith, who was the first to publish the work in the United States. Perhaps Smith coined the phrase after reading Nentvig's inscription on the final page of the Mexico City manuscript, which reads: "Descripción Geográfica, Natural y Curiosa de la Provincia de Sonora por un amigo de el servicio de Dios y de el Rey Nuestro Señor. Año de 1764." Translated, this is: "A crude [raw, unfinished, rough] and curious geographic description of the province of Sonora [written] by a friend in the service of God and our Lord the King, the year of 1764."

And, too, Smith must have noted the informality of the author's writing style. For example, Nentvig concludes his remarks at the end of section two, chapter ix, with the plea, "I beg the benevolent reader to forgive the disarray of the last two sections of this chapter." The title *Rudo Ensayo* seems even more apropos in light of the later discovery of Father Nentvig's letter of February 14, 1765,[1] to Provincial

---

[1] Located in the Temporalidades section, legajo 17–24, Archivo Histórico de Hacienda, Mexico City, as is the July 16, 1764 letter to Zeballos cited in this preface.

Francisco Zeballos, S.J., in which Nentvig pens, "The Description is badly arranged." Today, the *Rudo Ensayo* title of Smith's version is well accepted and synonymous with the work.

The authorship of the manuscript was in question for many years. Because the author referred to himself on the title page of the Mexico City manuscripts as "a friend of the common good" and on the final page as "one in the service of God and our Lord the King," investigators believed the writer to be connected with the church. And since the Jesuits were the sole religious group responsible for the province of Sonora, it was believed the author had to be a Jesuit priest. Buckingham Smith, as well as other investigators, suspected the Jesuit missionary Juan Nentvig, but definite proof was not obtained until February, 1950, when a docket of letters was found in the Archivo Histórico de Hacienda of Mexico, Temporalidades section, legajo 17-24.[2] In a postscript to this letter to Zeballos, Nentvig wrote:

> Concerning the Descripción de Sonora, it had to be ready within a very limited time: before the departure of Señor Tienda de Cuervo [December 9, 1762]. The Descripción is badly arranged. I wrote it surreptitiously during the summer when my health was not so good. Lacking necessary data, I requested information from various individuals who paid no attention to my appeals ... I would prefer that less credit be given to me alone for the writing of such an important work as the history of this province, to which I would gladly dedicate my efforts in a more thorough manner were it not for my endless occupations ... and my blindness has prevented me from reviewing my notes ...[3]

With reference to Tienda de Cuervo one is able to establish the year in which the essay was written. But the Madrid manuscript bears the date 1763 while the two Mexico City manuscripts are dated 1764. An explanation seems in order.

[2] Pradeau, A. F. "Description of Sonora," *Mid-America,* **24,** new series no. 2, (April 1953): 81–90.

[3] Father Nentvig, writing to Father José Hidalgo, S.J., October 5, 1766, states that in order to see better he was using the glasses of the deceased Father Tomás Pérez de la Busta, S.J.

In the middle of 1762 Spain was at war with England. The British had captured Havana, and the governor of Sonora, Don José Tienda de Cuervo, a lieutenant colonel in the Regiment of Dragoons, was ordered by the viceroy of New Spain to report for active duty with his regiment at Veracruz. Tienda de Cuervo left Sonora December 9, 1762, carrying a copy of the essay and corresponding map, to which Nentvig referred in another letter to Provincial Zeballos, this one dated July 16, 1764, and appearing in translation in this volume. One learns from this that another manuscript was carried by Father Visitor Ignacio Lizassoian, S.J., who left Sonora September 23, 1762, and forwarded the work to Mexico City from Charcos de Celaya, state of Guanajuato, December 13, 1762. Since the manuscript carried by Tienda de Cuervo was intended for the viceroy, who apparently had requested such an essay, it would seem safe to assume that Cuervo was carrying the original and Lizassoian, a copy. Because of the death of Cuervo, the original never reached the viceroy and its whereabouts is unknown. The copy carried by Lizassoian, intended for Nentvig's superior, reached Mexico City, and from it at least one copy was made during the early part of 1763 and sent to Madrid. Other copies were made less hurriedly in Mexico City, amending and updating the essay to correspond with more recent information. For example, the Mexico City manuscripts record the death of Curate Juan José de Grijalva in January, 1763, but the Madrid manuscript makes no mention of it. This leads to the belief that the manuscripts do not bear the date in which the essay was written but rather the year in which each was copied or amended.

Buckingham Smith apparently examined the two manuscripts in Mexico City as well as the one in Madrid, for he served as chargé d'affaires for the United States in Mexico from 1850 to 1851 and later traveled to Spain. Since Smith used the 1763 date of the Madrid manuscript on his version, one might assume he followed the Madrid text.

Comparing the Smith text with the Mexico City manuscript used in this interpretation, one discovers some interesting and significant differences that prove the Mexico City manuscripts were written later. The missionary assignments given in the Smith text are confirmed in the yearly Jesuit provincial catalogue of 1762, while the missionary assignments in the Mexico City manuscripts coincide with the yearly

Jesuit provincial catalogue of 1764. The following chart lists the placements of missionaries as given in Smith's text dated 1763 and the Mexico manuscripts dated 1764:

1763		1764
Jacobo Sedelmayr	Tecoripa	Francisco Javier González
José Joaquín Franco	Cumuripa	Benito Antonio Romeo
Guillermo David Borio	Mátape	Jacobo Sedelmayr
José Toral	Banámichi	Francisco Javier Villaroya
Salvador de la Peña	Opodepe	Ignacio Pfefferkorn
Ignacio Pfefferkorn	Guevavi	Custodio Jimeno

Then, too, chronological discrepancies are found in other areas. In chapter v, section one, Nentvig alludes to the thirteen years he has been in the northwest. Since he arrived in 1750, 1762 would be his thirteenth year in the province. Yet, in his letter of December 3, 1754, to the visitor general José Utrera,[4] Nentvig states he took charge of the Saric Mission, his first in Sonora, on June 21, 1751. However, the yearly Jesuit provincial catalogue has him there in 1750. In chapter vi, section three, the good father refers to the encounter between the Spanish forces and the Seris in "November or December of this past year, 1761." Since the manuscripts record events that occurred in 1763 and 1764, the 1761 date here seems puzzling. The Smith text states that the depopulation of Cananea took place in 1762, while the Mexico City manuscripts, chapter ix, section two of this interpretation, give 1763 as the date.

The manuscript used for this interpretation is in the Archivo General de la Nación (Mexico), history section, volume 393. There are other known manuscripts. They are in the Real Academia de la Historia, Madrid; the Huntington Library, San Marino, California; and another in the Archivo General de la Nación (Mexico), volume 16.

The first Spanish version was published in *Documentos para la*

---

[4] Located in the Archivo Franciscano, Biblioteca Nacional, caja 33–692, Mexico City, it was published in *Documentos para la historia de México,* **1,** second series, pp. 195–204.

historia de México, volume **XVI,** pages 489–616, Mexico, 1853–1856. The second was by Buckingham Smith, St. Augustine, Florida, 1863; a third published version is identical as far as it goes to the *Documentos para la historia* but is incomplete in the *Boletín del Archivo General de la Nación* (Mexico), volumes **XXVI** (1955), **XXVIII** (1957), **XXIX** (1958). Furthermore, there is an English version by Eusebio Guiteras printed by the American Catholic Historical Society of Philadelphia in 1894 and republished by Arizona Silhouettes, Tucson, Arizona, 1951. More recently, a fourth version, in Spanish and modified to some extent by Germán Viveros, was published by the Archivo General de la Nación of Mexico, second series, number 1, 1971.

An important item in Nentvig's correspondence relates to the existence of a map that goes along with the essay. Nentvig wrote in his letter to Zeballos, July 16, 1764:

> I have just replied to a letter from His Excellency the Viceroy dated May 19 [1764], in which he asks me for a map of this province. I had one left, identical to the one carried by the deceased Tienda de Cuervo but not so well finished.

And to the viceroy, the Marquis de Cruillas, Nentvig wrote on July 15, 1764:

> As we do not have the necessary instruments nor the ability to use them, the map was not made by mathematical observations. Instead, it was drawn following the knowledge acquired on my travels through Sonora and the Pimería, adding the information obtained from experts on the Apache and Seri lands.[5]

On February 14, 1765, Nentvig wrote to Zeballos:

> I have just received the very esteemed letter of November 15, 1764, in which Your Reverence embarrasses me by granting me more credit than I deserve. Permit me to confess that my part in the preparation of the map was limited to making a

[5] Located in the Archivo General de la Nación, Mexico City, Provincias internas section, vol. **86,** folios 332–3.

> rough sketch. It was Father Middendorff who drew and finished it so beautifully. Therefore, if it has any merit, the credit should go to him.

As for the copy of the essay and map carried by Tienda de Cuervo, one can well surmise why it was not delivered to the viceroy, who at the time had gone to Veracruz to make preparations for the expected attack by the British. Cuervo either contracted smallpox in Mexico City or fell ill and died in the unwholesome climate of Veracruz shortly after his arrival. Referring to the map, Nentvig wrote to Zeballos (February 14, 1765) that it was "... taken by Tienda de Cuervo ... and upon his death his widow took it to Spain, and I fear she will have it published there ..." The cartouche in the lower left corner of the map reads:

> Chorographic draft of Sonora and Pimería, Provinces of North America from the 26 degree to the 36 degree latitude and from the 257 degree to the 269 degree longitude of the Tenerife meridian, drawn from the sketch made by Father Juan Nentvig of the Society of Jesus and presented to His Excellency the Marquis of Cruillas, Viceroy, Governor and Captain General, etc. of New Spain.

Within the elaborately embellished cartouche and just below the above quoted legend is a code of symbols representing presidios, missions in ruin, principal or head missions, dependent missions, mining settlements, ranches, colonies of white inhabitants, towns with large numbers of Spaniards, water holes, Indian villages, and mine shafts as well as devastated towns.

In the lower right corner—a region not included in the essay—is an illustration of a castle being cannonaded, perhaps the sketcher's memory of a European siege.

A reproduction of the Nentvig-Middendorff map is included in this interpretation, thanks to the trustees of the British Museum who very kindly supplied a copy of the original in their possession and granted permission (March 20, 1964) for its use. The map was believed lost. Fortunately, with the invaluable assistance of Father Ernest J. Burrus, S.J., the precious cartographic chart was located in the British Museum catalogued under *M*entuig, R53/1207, ADD 3424

OB. It was later published by Father Burrus in *La obra cartográfica de la provincia mexicana de la Compañía de Jesús 1567–1767,* volume **2,** chart number 39, Madrid version.

The original is 76 x 91.5 centimeters and badly stained. It is torn around the folds, and there are sizable portions missing, no doubt caused by lack of materials to wrap it properly for its long journey, rain in transit, and old age. Nentvig foresaw a certain amount of damage when he wrote in his letter of July 15, 1764, to the Marquis de Cruillas, "The map is being sent wrapped as well as circumstances permit to protect it from the prevailing rains."

The reproduction included in this version is reduced in size and has been carefully retouched without changing the spelling or altering the style of script.

Nentvig's descriptions of plants and animals often lack sufficient information for proper identification. Efforts were made to identify them, giving wherever possible their English equivalents and botanical or zoological nomenclature. In this area we are indebted to Mr. Howard E. Gulick for his praiseworthy cooperation, so generously offered.

Spelling varies indiscriminately in the manuscripts, *b* being used for *v* (and vice versa); *g* for *h*; and *c, s,* and *z* are frequently used interchangeably. The suffixes of *tze* and *tzi* often appear as *che* or *chi*, and the final letter *a* is at times omitted. Even among scholars today there is not agreement concerning the spellings of many villages, towns, and tribes, particularly when these are no longer in existence or now bear different names. In the interest of uniformity and clarity the translators have selected generally accepted spellings and used them uniformly throughout. Also in the interest of uniformity and clarity, the translators have added titles to chapters i, viii, and ix, which are not titled in the manuscripts.

The Smith text, the Guiteras translation, and the Mexico manuscript were studied and compared. In this phase our departed friend Harmon J. Middaugh was an invaluable aid, and his assistance is gratefully acknowledged.

Even though Nentvig was terribly busy, indisposed, enduring the heat of the summer, and suffering from failing eyesight, he tended to be verbose; his syntax led to some confusion in many instances, even for persons well versed in the language and region. The goal of this interpretation, then, is to render Father Nentvig's essay in readable English and clarify ambiguous points by offering a free translation in keeping with his meaning.

In the preparation of this interpretation the writings of Nentvig's contemporaries—Kino, Pérez Ribas, Pfefferkorn, Roxas, Sedelmayr, etc.—were consulted and compared with accounts of modern writers. The Nentvig-Middendorff map was closely followed, and annotations that might prove useful were made throughout the text. Brackets were used to set off explanatory notes by the translators within the text, and footnotes have been added by us to help clarify and amplify points for the reader, and perhaps to open avenues for further investigation.

ALBERTO FRANCISCO PRADEAU
ROBERT R. RASMUSSEN

Biographical Sketch

Juan Nentvig (Jean Nentwich, Johann Nentvig) (Nentwig, Nentoig, Hispanicized Nentuig)

Born in Schlessen, Germany, which is now Klodzko, Poland, on March 28, 1713, Juan Nentvig entered the Society of Jesus presumably at Glatz, Bohemia, August 28, 1734, and ended his studies there in 1744. Most investigators cite the 1744 date as the beginning of his Jesuit college life. But the records are quite clear that he was a priest in 1750. Taking into consideration the ten-year probationary period required to become a Jesuit, one must conclude that the 1744 date signals the end of Nentvig's college life rather than its beginning.

In letters and other writings Father Nentvig's name appears in several forms. Probably baptized Johann Nentwich, he has also been called Nentwig and Nentoig, as well as Nentvig. Too, his name has been hispanicized Juan Nentuig. Also, his first name is sometimes listed as Jean. Juan Nentvig is used throughout this interpretation because it appears to be the name most widely accepted.

Choosing to become a missionary, Nentvig applied and obtained permission to go to the West Indies. He left what is now Prague, Czechoslovakia, January 28, 1749, and arrived at the Hospício, or temporary housing for Jesuits, of Santa María de Cádiz on May 12. From 1767 to 1772 this same hospício served as a detention camp for the exiled members of the Order, and the building still stands today on Topete Street, but it is no longer church property.

On June 17, 1750, he sailed for New Spain on *El Corazón de Jesús,* a French trading ship also known as *El Conde.* Accompanying him were 43 pious souls under the charge of Father Vicente de Vera, S.J.

The embarkation papers (contratación vouchers) describe Nentvig as a full-fledged priest, 36 years old, tall, slender, and dark skinned with brown hair.

Encountering favorable winds, *El Corazón de Jesús* arrived in Veracruz in record time, docking on August 25. From there Nentvig traveled immediately to Mexico City, where it is recorded he visited the mint. Shortly thereafter he received an assignment to the main mission of Tubutama in the northwest of New Spain.

In Sonora there were rumblings of discontent, and the 37-year-old priest was reassigned to Sáric. In 1751 the catalogues of the Jesuit Order register him as having completed his studies and describe him as being robust, with a pensive nature and sound judgment.

The tremendous rebellion that began on November 21, 1751, caught Nentvig in Sáric, but he managed to escape when Father Sedelmayr, S.J., notified him that his life was in danger if he were to stay there. Nentvig reached Tubutama, where he, Father Sedelmayr, and a handful of followers defended the mission church for two days. Despite a head contusion that made him delirious, Nentvig managed to reach Santa Ana five days later.

Without an official assignment, he officiated at Santa María Suamca until March 18, 1753, at which time he was sent to Tecoripa where he remained until March 15, 1757. Then he was transferred to the principal mission of Huásabas (Guásabas) where he took his fourth vow on February 2, 1759, and was appointed superior in 1763. Because the Regional Visitor, Father Manuel Aguirre, S.J., was in poor health, Father Nentvig assisted him in the duties of that office until 1767.

It was in Huásabas that Nentvig wrote the *Descripción de Sonora*. He found time to finish it during the summer of 1762 in the midst of a smallpox epidemic when he was burdened with the task of caring for the ailing fathers Aguirre and Och and weighed down with his regular priestly duties. Compounding his difficulties was failing eyesight. No glasses were available until years later. It wasn't until February, 1766, upon the death of Father Tomás Pérez de la Busta, S.J., of Sahuaripa, that Father Nentvig began using the glasses of the deceased father.

While in Huásabas, Father Nentvig reconstructed the mission church, furnishing it with silver accessories and splendid altar ornaments. Although the Apaches laid siege to the town frequently, Father Nentvig managed to raise good crops, breed about one thousand head of cattle, and keep his mission free of debt. Furthermore, the mission contributed generously to the native garrison guarding the community and to the Elizondo Expedition to Sonora.[1] During his last months in Huásabas, he applied for and received the assistance of Father Ramón Sánchez, S.J.

As visitor-rector, Father Nentvig ordered the Jesuit ministers in his district to travel to Mátape in obedience to the governor's edict of July 14, 1767, where they were informed of their banishment.[2] Meekly they marched to San José de Guaymas and, after a stay of a few months, embarked on the packet ship *El Principe* to Matanchel. From this port they traveled by land to Guadalajara, a terminus Father Nentvig never reached, for he died at Ixtlán on September 11, 1768, and was buried a day or so later at Jala (Xala), municipality of Santa María del Oro, county of Ahuacatlán, state of Nayarit.

Historian Donald C. Cutter searched for Father Nentvig's grave in Jala unsuccessfully in 1967. It would appear that the good father's final resting place has been lost forever.

---

[1] In an effort to quell Indian raids within the province, the Elizondo expeditionary force of about 1,100 men led by Colonel Domingo Elizondo was sent to Sonora in May, 1768, and remained until April, 1771. Cf. Almada's *Diccionario ...*, pp. 259–60.

[2] The governor's instrucción of July 14, 1767, is quoted verbatim in Pradeau's *Expulsión de los Jesuitas de las provincias de Sonora, Ostimuri y Sinaloa*, pp. 41–4.

Letter from Nentvig to Zeballos (July 16, 1764)

My Beloved Father Provincial Francisco Zeballos, ✝ Pax Christy

I have just replied to a letter from His Excellency the Viceroy dated May 19th, in which he asks me for a map of this province. I had one left, identical to the one carried by the deceased Tienda de Cuervo but not so well finished. Because the Viceroy's request demanded urgency, I sent it as it was. My vision is poor, and without glasses to improve it, I would have blurred the chart had I tried to amend it.

I attempted to explain this to His Excellency, but not being familiar with court etiquette nor with the style used with such personages, I fear that unknowingly I may have committed some error and displeased him, and I may have made matters worse by refusing to furnish information about the latest incidents with our enemies although I did say that day by day, in spite of the precautions taken by the governor, the Seri and Apache Indians are gaining on us, the former having killed nine soldiers at Aigame. These are matters upon which His Excellency would be more thoroughly informed [than I].

I did not have anything worthwhile to call to His Excellency's attention although I had heard that the governor had issued orders to the captain and his soldiers at Fronteras to join in a foray against the Seris and Pimas at Cerro Prieto. But not knowing this with certainty, I did not mention it.

Being overburdened with work, I have had no time for soliciting data. Father Och, who, because of his hernia, left Bacerac on orders from the Father Visitor, is now here awaiting an easier assignment, and were it not for his presence I do not know how I could care for so many afflicted with smallpox, more than sixty in Oputo alone, and just as many, whom Father Och is attending physically as well as spiritually, in Guásabas, eleven leagues away. Without his care most of them would have died.

My reply to the Viceroy was in the penmanship of Father Och which is very good. I mention this to Your Reverence in case the Viceroy is offended, in which case you might send someone to explain my awkwardness. I also request instructions from Your Reverence on how to proceed if in the future similar information which we have been forbidden to impart is requested. I do not wish to trample on statutes and precepts, even if they are interpreted in a less strict manner, nor do I care to undertake superfluously another's work.

I shall rejoice if Your Reverence is enjoying good health; thanks be to The Lord I am well. I continue praying to God, on whose Sacred Sacraments I commit myself, that you will be with us many years.

Oputo, July 16, 1764.

The humblest servant and vassal of Your Reverence,

Juan Nentvig

P.S. I failed to mention that in order to comply better with the wishes of the Viceroy, I cited the last chapter of the description of Sonora carried by Señor Tienda de Cuervo without letting him know that I had written it. I am sure he will agree with me that it would be expedient to subdue and punish the enemies of Sonora. If by chance the description were not in the hands of the Viceroy, Your Reverence could order that a copy be made from the one sent to you some time ago with Father Ignacio Lissassoayn [sic], at least such portions that in Your Reverence's judgment should be seen by the Viceroy, who seems well disposed and might decide with earnestness upon the needed war.

Source: Translated from Temporalidades section, vouchers 17–24, Archivo Histórico de Hacienda, Mexico City.

Rudo Ensayo

I

A Description of Sonora

SECTION ONE

Its Name, Location, and Boundaries

It appears that this region was named Sonora from the beginning. The name was first given to either the principal valley or the old mining district of San Juan Bautista de Sonora, seat of the curacy, abandoned at present, not because its rich ores have been exhausted, but partly because the shafts were flooded and partly because of the incessant hostilities of the Apaches.

Although I know nothing of the etymology or origin of the name Sonora, I do not believe I am deceiving myself in being inclined to think it may have been suggested by her great wealth, the news of which swept sonorously across New Spain and into Europe. Perhaps the name might have been given accidentally as has been the case with other provinces of the New World. Still, Sonora, in spite of being assailed by the Apaches, has not failed, nor is she now failing, to conform to the prophecy of the poet who wrote *Conveniunt rebus nomina saepe suis.*[1] And as the sound waves of gold and silver spread, so has the fame of Sonora, for there is no portion of this province that does not offer these precious metals, almost on the surface, to those who have the patience to dig and separate the ore from the dirt, or, as it were, the wheat from the chaff. There is an inexhaustible source of these and other metals.

Sonora is located in North America, in the vice-royalty of New

[1] "Names oftentimes fit their objects."

Spain, under the judicial administration of the royal court of Guadalajara, New Galicia. Ecclesiastically it is dependent upon the Durango diocese and it is under the governorship of Sinaloa, an administrative region divided into six provinces: Chametla, Copala, Culiacán, Sinaloa, Ostimuri, and Sonora. Though Sonora is the last in the order of conquest and farthest in location, it is definitely foremost, not only of the provinces named but possibly of all the others in this vast Mexican empire because of the fertility of the soil, its rich mines and placers, and the docility of the natives—chiefly the Opata and Eudebe tribes whose languages differ but slightly. These tribes compete with one another to show their affection for Christianity and their fidelity to our monarchs to whose rule they have submitted voluntarily as related by Father Andrés Pérez Ribas, S.J., in his work *Historia de los triunfos de Nuestra Santa Fe entre las gentes mas bárbaras y fieras del Nuevo Orbe.*[2]

Its boundaries are as follows: on the east, a 30-league-wide range of mountains, the Sierra Madre Occidental, separating it from the Tarahumara country; on the west, the Gulf of California from the mouth of the Yaqui River on the south to that of the Colorado River on the north; the correct boundary on the south would be the right bank of the Yaqui River except the portion northeast of Cumuripa where it takes a portion of the province of Ostimuri in order to cover the four Jesuit missions of Movas, Nuri, Onavas, and Tónichi that are on the left bank; on the north its boundary begins on the east from Bacerac and extends for seventy leagues west through the presidios of Fronteras to Terrenate, but in order to include the Pimería Alta the line must be extended north from Fronteras to the junction of the San Pedro and Gila rivers. From this point the boundary follows the course of the Gila River for a distance of 130 leagues westward to where it joins the Colorado River, thus separating the Pimería Alta from innumerable heathen nations inhabiting the vast unknown land to the north, and according to the writings of Father Eusebio Francisco Kino who crossed that great river at the urgings of those nations, their tribesmen were affable, docile, and humane.[3]

---

[2] Madrid, 1645. A more recent edition in three volumes: Mexico, 1944.

[3] Father Kino crossed the river on October 2, 1700, as recorded in Bolton's *Kino's Historical Memoir of Pimería Alta,* **I:**246.

The northern boundary has been placed at those rivers even though there are many heathens among the Papagos, Gila, Pimas, Cocomaricopas, Yumas, etc. who live on the southern bank to whom the Gospel has been preached by the Jesuit missionaries fathers Kino, Ignacio Javier Keller, and Jacobo Sedelmayr who have visited the valleys along those rivers many times with much industry and without assistance from the Royal Treasury except their salaries.[4] Thus they have won for the Church and the Monarchy from Culiacán to San Xavier del Bac and Tucson in the Pimería Alta more than two hundred leagues. This does not include the land they conquered under similar circumstances in Lower California and other provinces.

SECTION TWO

Its Latitude and Longitude

Concerning the geographical location of Sonora, we do not have the necessary instruments nor the tranquility needed to take exact observations because of the incessant Apache raids. Therefore it has been advisable to avail ourselves of information gathered by missionaries in different parts of the province. Their data and the known distances between places permitted the figuring of approximate geographical locations. We hope that our predicament may serve as an incentive to others to obtain more accurate ones. So, assuming our computations to be correct, we place the mouth of the Yaqui River at 26 degrees, 24 minutes northern latitude and having no ships to explore the western boundary we prefer to omit the variations of longitude rather than to err. The mouth of the Colorado River is placed at 33 degrees, 30 minutes, and if we advance northward another degree we reach the junction of the Gila and the Colorado, which fixes the outermost point beyond which there is nothing more, at 34 degrees, 30 minutes northern latitude. There is a distance of 8 degrees, 6 minutes, or 162 leagues from north to south.

---

[4] Before 1608 the salaries were 250 pesos yearly per individual. In 1608 they were raised to 300 pesos a year. This varied, however, with the more inaccessible areas getting larger salaries. Furthermore, each mission received a yearly allowance of 129 pesos for general expenses. When a missionary visited his district or was transferred to another rectorship, he was reimbursed for his traveling expenses.

The computation of longitudes is a more arduous task which we have not been able to determine by correspondence. The few instruments we had, obtained from Europe to record the lunar eclipse forecast by a Jesuit for 1751, were lost during the Pima uprising of 1751. The computation of longitudes is so important in a geographical description, and our aim in this short essay is limited to and by available material. Therefore we hope that the benevolent reader will not denounce our effort as presumptuous but instead magnanimously praise our daring. We shall not count from the first meridian to ours through the continents of Europe, Asia, and the intervening seas to the American Continent, but instead deduct from the 360-degree meridian proportionately by leagues, and by this method I have determined from Tenerife to the mouth of the Colorado River is more or less 258 degrees longitude, and the Yaqui River is 263 degrees, 42 minutes. The mountain range from Yécora through Taraichi, Chamada, Sátechi, and Tamichopa to the Carretas slopes is 268 degrees longitude, giving us 10 degrees difference in longitude from the mouth of the Colorado River to Taraichi, not in a straight line west to east but from northwest to southeast according to the direction of the coastline of the Gulf of California.

II

On the Rivers and Brooks of Sonora

SECTION ONE

The Yaqui River and Its Tributaries

The Yaqui is the first and most copious of Sonora's rivers. Its origin is in the western slopes of the Sierra Madre Occidental, emerging at the abandoned estancia[1] of Tamichopa. A league and a half to the west it receives the waters of the Guachinera Brook, and two leagues beyond it receives the water of the Bavispe Brook. It then makes a sharp turn northward, flowing between mountains. Eighteen leagues northwest of Bavispe it is joined by two streams which unite to form one. One stream has its origin at three marshy springs near Teuricachi and Cuchuta. The waters from these three springs join with the flows from a spring east of Cuquiárachi and a fifth spring near Fronteras.

After receiving the waters from these streams, the river flows northward then turns east, making a long curve, and at about eight or nine leagues beyond, it is joined by the Cabullona and San Bernardino streams in the Batepito Valley. The enlarged river then takes a southern course, curving along the way through the depopulated mining settlements of Teras, San Juan del Río and Nori, watering the lands of Oputo and Huásabas.

For twenty-eight leagues south of Batepito Valley the river receives no tributaries except small drainings from the mountains it skirts, and most of the year even these are nonexistent. The result is that from May through July the river known as Río Grande is usually

[1] Originally meaning cattle ranch, estancia later meant an overnight shelter for travelers, synonymous with puesto.

dry except for a few potholes until six or seven leagues south of Huásabas. There it is joined by a creek that rises in the vicinity of Bacadéhuachi. The flow continues southward for about twenty leagues, narrowing because of its proximity to the mountains.

Near the ruined town of San Mateo the Mulatos River discharges its waters into the Grande. The Mulatos has its origin in the Sierra Madre Mountains in the land of Tarahumara between Maicoba and Moris, and after numerous bends on its westward course, it is joined by the Aros and other creeks. It merges into open country between Sátechi and Chamada, irrigating a few corn patches which are frequently lost because of flood or drought. At this juncture the river can be forded if it is not swollen. Otherwise it is necessary to use rafts which the San Mateo natives make and handle skillfully. At the ford the river is joined by a small brook coming from the slopes of Plomosa Hill some fourteen leagues to the east. Farther south it receives a larger stream arising around Taraichi, fourteen leagues southeast. This stream irrigates the areas of Onapa, Pónida, and Sahuaripa.

The Grande then assumes a slight westward course between mountain ranges to Todos Santos where it is joined by a river variously named according to the townships it supplies. This river arises north of Cumpas and is augmented by streams from springs at Jamaica, Jécori, Oposura, and Térapa and by a rivulet from Tepache. It winds southward through canyons to Batuc, and three leagues farther it merges with the Grande which continues without any tributaries for eighteen leagues, running between mountain ranges with fording places at Soyopa, San Francisco, and San Antonio, each but a short distance from the other. All these are on the right bank. The river then makes a slight turn to the southeast, the town of Tónichi being on the left bank. Close by, the river receives water from a creek that arises in the Milpillas Mountains, twelve leagues to the east.

Five leagues farther south, the Grande has Onabas on its left, and eight leagues farther south it receives the waters of the Río Chico Stream which has its beginning at the mining settlement of Santísima Trinidad. The stream flows southwest of Nuri. It follows a westward course, irrigating the fields of Movas and the mining settlement of Río Chico. Four leagues farther west it empties into the Grande which at this point turns southwest, having Cumuripa on its right bank.

On the same bank it receives the waters of the Tecoripa Brook that sprouts north of the town of the same name, irrigates its land and also that of the Suaqui and some of Cumuripa; then it joins the Grande. Twelve leagues southwest it reaches the Buenavista presidio, and from there the river is called Yaqui and assumes a more westerly course to water eight of the Yaqui settlements, seven being on its left bank.[2]

As in the case of the Nile, the Yaqui River irrigates the lands through which it runs from January to July. The Yaqui empties into the Gulf of California where now and then ships wait to transport much needed supplies to Lower California and to carry travelers to its pearl fisheries.

SECTION TWO

Of Other Rivers and Creeks

Many of the so-called rivers of this province are actually mediocre streams. While all have their courses directed toward the Gulf of California, none reaches it, and their waters disappear in the sand long before coming within sight of the coast. From east to west the first river after the Yaqui is the Mátape [29 degrees latitude, 265 degrees longitude] arising a short distance north of the mission of that name. Its volume is very scant, barely irrigating an orchard and plot of ten to twelve fanegas[3] of wheat and scarcely providing drinking water to the town, particularly during dry years. At Nácori, two leagues west, it is necessary to sink wells to obtain drinking water with little or none left for irrigation. The underground current of the Mátape reappears at Mazatán three leagues west, flows for a stretch, disappears, reappears at Cobaichi Springs only to vanish a short distance away. It surfaces again at San José de los Pimas in sufficient quantity to irrigate a plot planted with three or four fanegas of wheat, and then vanishes entirely. At the village of Alamos northwest of Mátape a thin trickle arises which disappears a short distance away. Another rivulet arises twelve leagues to the northeast, runs past the deserted farms of

[2] The eight Yaqui settlements are Cócorit, Bacum, Torim, Vicam, Potam, Rahum, Güíribis, and Belem.

[3] A measure equal to 1.6 bushels.

Batasaqui and Topisco, and after watering some fields to the west of the latter, it also disappears.

Next is the Sonora River, originating in the mining district of Cananea. Augmented by springs around the abandoned village of Mototicachi and drainings from the Mababi Mountains, it passes Bacoachi, Chinapa, and Güepavérachi and enters the Sonora Valley. There it is joined by a creek arising from several springs near the mining settlement of Bacanuchi and follows a southern course irrigating Arizpe, the deserted real[4] of Tetoachi, Sinoquipe, Motepore, Banámichi, Hüépac, the mining settlement of Sonora, Aconchi, Baviácora, the Concepción puesto[5] and the Núñez. All of these are on the left bank of the Sonora River which then turns west and irrigates Ures, the depopulated real of Gavilán, San José de Gracia, and the deserted village of San Francisco. Thirteen leagues farther west the Sonora is joined by the Opodepe River and waters the fields and vineyards of Pitic where it ends in dry years. But when the rains are excessive, it reaches Siete Cerritos and disappears in the sandy soil of Tenuage, not a drop reaching the Gulf of California.

The Opodepe is another small river and has its beginning at Saracachi [31 degrees latitude, 264 degrees longitude]. It is augmented by the marshy springs of Pueblo Viejo, at present a community of Spaniards, formerly the Dolores Mission. After receiving trickles from creeks at San Bruno and Chupi Sonora, it flows through a canyon five or six leagues long to Cucurpe then flows south to Toape. Still flowing south, it passes the real of San José on its right bank six

---

[4] This is Tercachi on Nentvig's map. *Real* as used here stands for real de minas, which means royal mining settlement, signifying that a small garrison of royal troops was stationed there for the protection of the site, not that it was the property of the Crown. Ecclesiastically all reales de minas were administered by diocesan ministers. Occasionally, and by request of the priest, members of the Jesuit order performed the rites, turning over the revenues or tithes to the diocesan minister. About 1664 the twenty-fifth viceroy of New Spain, Antonio Alvaro Sebastián de Toledo, Marquis of Mancera, decreed that reales de minas must be administered by the regular or secular priests. This meant that Jesuits in Sonora could not attend to them except by request as stated above.

[5] Puesto or estancia is usually a farm that served as an overnight shelter for travelers.

leagues distant. Opodepe is a league beyond, and Nacameri is seven leagues still further.

The river then turns slightly to the west supplying the Antúnez farm and two leagues beyond, Pópulo, formerly a Seri settlement. A league away it enters the royal presidio of San Miguel de Horcasitas[6] with the pueblo of Angeles immediately after. Four leagues farther on, the Opodepe reaches the good lands of Cerro Pelón,[7] and twelve leagues beyond, it joins the Sonora River.

The fourth river is the Cocóspera which has its origin in a spring near the mission of that name [32 degrees latitude, 264 degrees longitude]. It flow south and within a distance of three leagues receives the waters of a small creek arising at the depopulated Remedios settlement. It irrigates Imuris where its volume is increased by a small brook that rises at Sucurisutac, an abandoned ranch five leagues north of Imuris. Following a slightly southwesterly course, it proceeds to San Ignacio four leagues away and irrigates Santa María Magdalena two leagues farther south. It continues three leagues beyond through the deserted mining settlement of San Lorenzo and reaches Santa Ana five leagues farther on. All these settlements are on the left or eastern bank.

A short distance farther south the river makes a sharp turn to the west, and its waters disappear in the plains of Santa Rosa only to burst forth forty leagues away in the vicinity of Pitiquito[8] where it joins the Tubutama River which arises from a spring in Arizona [32 degrees, 14 minutes latitude, 263 degrees longitude]. Its waters run directly south through the real of Agua Caliente where the waters from its spring augment the Tubutama which continues to Aquimuri and beyond some three leagues further south where it is joined by a brook which descends from the marshes of Busani and irrigates Sáric two leagues away just before it joins the Aquimuri. About a league and a half

---

[6] Having San Miguel as patron saint, the presidio was named in honor of Viceroy Juan Francisco Güemes y Horcasitas. The presidio was founded and named by Visitor Judge with Executive Powers Don José Rafael Rodríguez Gallardo in 1749.

[7] This is Cuervo on Nentvig's map.

[8] This is Pitic on Nentvig's map.

before it reaches the town of Tubutama, the river receives the waters of a spring and on its southwesterly course supplies Santa Teresa, Atí, and Oquitoa, each about two leagues from the other. All are on the right bank. About two leagues farther, it passes the Altar presidio, and just before reaching Pitiquito it receives the waters of the resurgent Cocóspera. Then it irrigates the fields of Caborca. From there its meager waters waste away, disappearing near Busani some twenty-two leagues from the gulf.

The fifth river[9] emerges about a league northeast of Santa María Soamca [32 degrees, 30 minutes latitude, 264 degrees longitude] and flows south to San Lázaro then turns west to San Luis and Buenavista. From there it turns northwest to Guebavi, Calabazas, and Tumacacori, finally reaching the Tubac presidio where it ordinarily ends except when the rains are abundant. Then it flows farther north, skirting the Santa Rita Mountains, to San Xavier del Bac.

SECTION THREE

The Gila and the San Pedro Rivers

The San Pedro or Sobahipuris River has its origin about two leagues southeast of Terrenate. It flows northwest and is joined in about two leagues by a creek that rises north of Terrenate presidio, proceeds through the San Pedro Valley and the pleasant Sobahipuri Valley, irrigating their fields until it merges with the Gila at 33 degrees latitude [263 degrees, 30 minutes longitude].[10]

The Gila, this large river arising about 36 degrees latitude and 268 degrees longitude in the southern slopes of the Mogollon Mountains in Apache land, emerges from the straits of a long canyon at Todos Santos[11] and flows through the Santa Lucía Valley where it receives

---

[9] The Santa Cruz River, not named in the manuscript or shown on the map.

[10] Nentvig's map shows a tributary originating at the Sauz Springs. The tributary is not mentioned in the manuscript.

[11] This is not shown on Nentvig's map.

the waters from two brooks,[12] one from the north and another from the south. In some places throughout its length of over one hundred leagues it turns to circumvent mountain ranges, but the westerly direction prevails. It flows through the whole Apache land, and for more than twenty leagues it irrigates the fertile Florida Valley. Forty-six leagues from its point of origin, it is joined by the San Francisco River, the source of which is in the northern slopes of the Mogollon Mountains near the granaries of the Apaches. The granaries were discovered by Spanish troops on their way to Acome during the campaign of 1737. These storage places resembled wells carved in the rocky slopes and were well stocked with grain. The San Francisco flows in a southwesterly direction between rugged mountain ranges and joins the Gila at the start of the Florida Valley, about six leagues north of the salty marshes [Ciénega Salada]. Farther west and about ten leagues to the south of the Gila at the western tip of the Florida Mountains, the range which parallels the river throughout the Florida Valley, are the marshy springs named Ojos de Agua Cenagosa. Upon leaving the Florida Valley and Apache land, the Gila breaks through the mountains and is joined by the San Pedro. Twenty leagues farther west of this junction and one league south of its left bank is the Casa Grande,[13] named after Moctezuma. There is a tradition current among the Indians and the Spaniards that the Mexicas, on their long transmigration, rested there. The building is four stories high with the roof supported by cedar or tlascal[14] beams. Its walls are of a very solid material, seemingly of the best mortar. It has many rooms and living compartments of sufficient capacity to lodge a traveling court. Three leagues from this house there is another Casas Grandes on the north bank of the Gila, much dismantled, and from the ruins one can surmise that this house was larger than the first one. For some leagues around these houses, wherever one digs, one finds shards of fine

[12] The two brooks are the Ojo de los Alamos and the Aguaje de Santa Lucía.

[13] This is plural on Nentvig's map.

[14] *Tlascal* is the Aztec word for white cedar.

pottery of various colors, and from a large irrigating canal two leagues farther up that is still visible, one deduces that the dwellers were not at these places merely in transit. The channel could supply a large community with water and irrigate many leagues of those fruitful and beautiful plains.

About half a league from the first house on the same side of the Gila there is a lagoon that empties into a river. This lagoon, although small in size, has a depth greater than has been possible to determine by means of several ropes tied end to end.

The Pimas tell of another house of odd design and unusual construction that is to be found much farther up the river which, as drawn in the sand by the natives, is a kind of labyrinth similar to the sketch that follows:

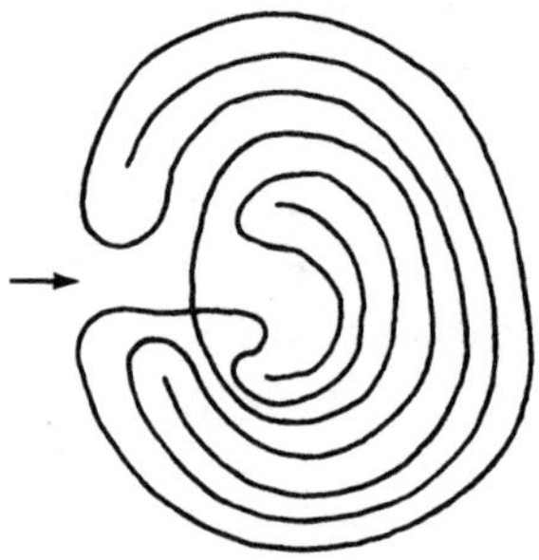

This seems more like a house of amusement than the residence of a grandee.

I have heard Father Ignacio Javier Keller, S.J., tell of other edifices, more spacious with better symmetry and finer art, which he had seen on his apostolic travels, although I do not remember where they were. He spoke of one that measures half a league in length on a straight line and nearly as much in depth. Divided into blocks, the remaining walls are three and four stories high but greatly dilapidated and collapsed in many places. It was a massive structure that resembled a castle. One corner is still standing. An irrigation canal was built in front of the building and was cleaved by many furrows and trenches through which water could drain into all streets, perhaps to clean them of filth as is done in Turín and other European cities and formerly in the city of Mexico. Doubtless Father Keller was referring to the Casas Grandes on the north bank of the Gila because those who have been there agree that the ruins are not of a single building but a large community.

The land between these houses on both banks of the Gila for a distance of ten leagues is inhabited by Pimas Altos called Gileños.

The mainland, as well as some islands within the river itself, is delightfully fruitful in wheat, corn, etc., and so much cotton that after the harvest, because of the apathy of the natives, more remains in the field, a fact recorded by a missionary in 1757.

Their irrigating canals, which bring the water from the river and some springs, were well constructed, the Indians having learned how to build them, no doubt, from Father Kino and other Jesuit missionaries who visited them from 1694 to 1751.

During the latter year the already converted Pimas rose in revolt, and by their bad example destroyed the well-founded hope that others could be brought into the fold. It is especially distressing, too, that the recently arrived missionaries had not applied the royal edict of December 4, 1747,[15] as the viceroy of New Spain instructed them to do.

The principal settlements along the Gila were, on the south side, Tucsonimó; on the north bank, Sudacson or Encarnación, which is the residence of Javanimó, their head chief; and farther west, the Santa Teresa hamlet with its abundant spring.

Ten or twelve leagues beyond these rancherías the Gila is joined by the Asunción River which, according to Father Jacobo Sedelmayr, S.J., is formed by the confluence of the Verde, so-called because of the verdant groves of poplars along its banks, and the Salado, so salty that for some distance after the Asunción joins the Gila the water remains undrinkable.

Ten leagues farther west of this junction the much enlarged Gila curves northwest and enters the land of the Opas and Cocomaricopas then resumes its westerly course. The Indian nations of the Opas and Cocomaricopas dwell on both sides of the river for a distance of 36 leagues. The hamlet of Tucsassic[16] is on the north side, while on the south side are Stucabitic, Ojia-taibues, Uparch, Tuquisán, and Sutac Sassaba, all with very rich soil.

---

[15] The royal edict of December 4, 1747, issued by Ferdinand VI, reiterated the edict of November 13, 1744, in which more adequate financial support for the missions and larger stipends for the missionaries were granted (cited in Bancroft's *North Mexican States,* p. 465, and Dunne's *Black Robes in Lower California,* pp. 316, 488). However, this was never put into effect in the northwest.

[16] This is Tucrapit on Nentvig's map.

Near the western end of this river and a short distance from the north bank there is an abundant hot water spring[17] where, according to a corporal in Father Sedelmayr's escort during the father's entry into the land of the Yumas in 1748, an Indian gave the missionary nuggets of pure silver as large as acorns, and when asked where they were found, the native pointed to a hill not far from Tumac, the last hamlet of the tribe.

From Tumac to the junction of the Colorado, a distance of forty leagues, there are no settlements along the course of the Gila. The Gila River ends where it joins the Colorado, some 250 leagues from its point of origin.

SECTION FOUR

The Colorado River

The Colorado River is the largest of the known rivers of North America discovered up till now. Nothing certain is known of its place of origin, but from its grandeur, breadth and depth, capable of admitting vessels of no mean dimensions, one deduces that its source must be far. Its course being from north to south has suggested to some that its origin is in the Canadian latitudes far to the west. If this is true, it would seem likely that it begins in the lakes on the banks of which the Mosemlec nation dwells as I remember having read in Andrés González Barcia's *Ensayo cronológico para historia general de la Florida*[18] where the author gives an account of a journey by Baron Lahontan, a Frenchman, to the Río Muerto where the Baron obtained information about New Mexico as well as the nation which he calls *Mozeemlekes*. Its locality, government and customs are similar to those of other civilized nations.[19] His account does not differ from that of Torquemada dealing with General Vázquez Coronado's entry of 1539.[20]

---

[17] Ojo de Agua Caliente.

[18] Madrid, 1723.

[19] Baron Lahontan was the king's lieutenant in Newfoundland. In 1690 he made a trip west of the Mississippi and sailed up a river that may have been the Missouri.

[20] *Monarquía Indiana*, **I**, book v, chapter xl, pp. 678–81.

Forty leagues north of the junction of the Gila and the Colorado the latter receives the waters of the Río Azul, not a large stream, that arises in the Moqui province three to four days march to the east, according to the natives. The left bank of the Colorado between these confluences has fertile soil and abundant springs. Furthermore, it is inhabited by the populous Hud-Coadan nation.

Just below the Colorado-Gila junction the former curves to the northwest and divides into branches leaving a portion of the land in the middle that may have prompted some geographers, even modern ones such as Monsieur [Nicolás Bras-de-Fer], to record the existence of a good-sized island. Even Father Kino refers to it as information given him by natives although he does not say he has seen it.[21]

The Yuma nation lives south of the Colorado-Gila junction for a distance of twelve leagues. In this I am in complete agreement with Fathers Kino and Sedelmayr.

The Cuhana nation makes its home with comfort on the left bank of a peninsula formed by the curving of the Colorado. The Quiquimas, the most numerous nation of all, dwell where the river resumes its southward course. This nation occupies a most fertile valley on the left bank for a distance of ten to twelve leagues extending to the very mouth of the Colorado where it enters the Gulf of California.

Father Sedelmayr affirms that the Pimas of the Gila, the Opas, the Cocomaricopas, the Hud-Coadans, Yumas, Cuhanas, and Quiquimas add up to 30,000 souls, and all speak the Pima language with only slight differences in dialect.[22]

---

[21] Father Kino did see Presentación Island. A letter from Father Kino to Father Leal dated April 8, 1702, and quoted by Bolton in his *Kino's Historical Memoir ...*, **I**, p. 350, states: "Also we learned and saw that the very large volumed Colorado River, a few leagues below the Río Grande or Hila, divided again into very large branches and with them makes a great island more than fifty leagues around with very fertile lands and very good plains."

[22] Apparently both Nentvig and Sedelmayr are mistaken here. Father Kino, in *Las Misiones*, p. 106, writes of visiting the Ranchería Grande on the Colorado River on February 22–23, 1699, and preaching to the three hundred inhabitants in Pima dialect as well as in the Yuma or Cocomaricopa tongue. Mange in *Luz de tierra incógnita*, p. 264, states that the Pimas and Yumas speak different languages. Corroborating this, Spicer in *Cycles of Conquest*, p. 263, classifies the Pima and Yuma dialects as two different tribal languages.

Nothing definite is known of the nations living on the west bank of the Colorado, only that there are many of them, and those nations are large. Father Kino, who crossed the river[23] at the urging of the natives, makes special mention of this in his diary. There the Quiquimas live, as do the Cuhanas, Coanopas, Ojiopas, etc., and they came to greet him at the residence of the Quiquima chieftain three leagues beyond the river. Father Kino describes their land as having rich soil which is well plowed, fallowed, sown, and planted with many beautiful trees. Furthermore, he said that the river had a width of two hundred rods at the fording place and was of immeasurable depth except at its banks at a point six to eight leagues from the gulf.

The Colorado abounds with fish of many varieties not identified by Father Kino although he tells of having been presented with so many that he and Father Manuel González,[24] now dead, did not know what to do with them.

The rivers and creeks of this province abound in catfish [*Bagre panamensis*] and a variety of white fish called matelote[25] [*Perca fluviatus*], savory but with so many tiny spines that it cannot be eaten without running the risk of having one of the spines wedge in one's throat.

In some streams there is also a kind of trout similar in color and markings to the trout found in Europe but not so savory.

Water turtles are not lacking, but neither the Indians nor the Spaniards eat them because they are judged ugly and wretched creatures. Some crabs and shrimp may be found, particularly in the Rio Grande south of Soyopa. Also there are many mullets. The Yaqui River is even more abundant in these and other varieties of more

[23] November 21, 1701.

[24] Father Manuel González, S.J., superior at Oposura and Cumpas, became ill on the trip along the Colorado and succumbed at Tubutama shortly after April 6, 1702. In January, 1712, his remains were removed and reinterred under the main altar at the San Francisco Javier chapel [Magdalena] by the side of Kino, his friend and companion.

[25] This fresh water fish may be the dardo or raño which Velázquez de la Cadena in his dictionary describes as full of spines. In some areas, in Cuchuvérachi for example (see note 41 in chapter ix), *matelote* is the regional name for róbalo.

delicate fish, such as róbalos [bream or black-snook, *Centropomus nigrescens* which in some places is called matelote], dorados [gilt-head, *Sparus aureatus* or dolphin, *Coriphaena hippurus*], salmon, etc., that occasionally come into the rivers from the sea because they like fresh water, especially at points where there is no menace of fierce alligators or crocodiles, for these play havoc with them.

III

Mountains, Climate, and Fertility of the Soil

SECTION ONE

Mountain Ranges

Sonora is mountainous, rugged, and uncultivated except for some small valleys, most of which are no more than glens measuring here and there from half a league to one or more in width. These valleys in nearly all instances extend from north to south, paralleling the mountain ranges that form them, as do the brooks or rivulets that irrigate them as described in the preceding chapter.

There are six mountain ranges extending from north to south. If a line were drawn from Nácori Chico on the east [30 degrees, 40 minutes latitude, 267 degrees, 20 minutes longitude] to San Miguel de Horcasitas on the west [30 degrees latitude, 263 degrees, 30 minutes longitude], all six ranges would cross it. As they approach the coast their height and mass decrease except in a few places, forming an imaginary stairway starting at the eastern boundary—the Sierra Madre Occidental—and ending at the western boundary—the Gulf of California.

The most prominent peaks along the coast of the Gulf of California are the Cerro Prieto [28 degrees, 10 minutes latitude, 263 degrees, 20 minutes longitude] and Picú [in the Carrizal Range at 30 degrees latitude, 261 degrees longitude], Las Espuelas and Bacoachi el Grande [30 degrees, 5 minutes latitude, 272 degrees, 20 minutes longitude], all in Seri land. The Santa Clara volcano—inactive—and some others are in the Pimería Alta.[1]

[1] These are not on Nentvig's map. They are located southwest of Sonoitac, ca. 32 degrees, 5 minutes latitude, 261 degrees, 5 minutes longitude.

The first range of mountains is the Nácori. Between the village of that name and Bacadéhuachi it forms a very limited dale which for want of irrigation is used only for seasonal planting. From this the Opatas of Nácori Chico and the Jovas of Mochopa eke out an existence.

The second range is that of Bacadéhuachi which, with six or seven leagues of rugged slopes and precipices, forms with the preceding range the little valley of Bacadéhuachi, three to four leagues long with a few bits of watered land and a small flour mill half a league from Bacadéhuachi powered by the small brook of the same name.

The third range unites with the second to enclose the Huásabas Valley with the Río Grande flowing through. This vale, though narrow, is fifty leagues in length extending from Batepito on the north to five leagues below Huásabas with no towns in between except Oputo, its dependent mission.[2] Because the population of this area is small and the Apache harassment great, one-tenth of the food-producing lands which the valley has to offer cannot be cultivated. These ranges extend on the north far into the region of the Apaches, and it is said by those who have been there that they reach the Chiguicagui Mountains[3] [34 degrees, 30 minutes latitude, 264 degrees longitude] and beyond to the Florida Range that skirts the Gila and reaches the San Pedro River. All that area is where the wild, reckless, and uncontrolled activities of the enemy, the Apaches, take place. The Florida Range and the fourth range form the Oposura Valley,[4] which is not so narrow as the ones described, affords much more comfort, allowing its inhabitants to breathe and enjoy more air and sunlight. While limited in length, it offers many bountiful fields to its tillers so that this valley alone, so well watered by a constantly running stream,

---

[2] Nori and San Juan del Río are not mentioned although they are in this area.

[3] In Opata, Chiguicagui means mountain of the guajolotes, or wild turkeys. It is spelled Chiguicagui on Nentvig's map, but the most commonly accepted spelling is Chiricahua. Other variants include Chihuicagui and Chiricahui.

[4] Actually, the valley is formed with just the northern portion of the fourth range joining the third one from Térapa to Cumpas.

could supply the Sonora Province with grain if there were more natives willing to serve the owners of the land.

The fourth range is less rugged and of lower height than the preceding ones. It forms a valley thirty leagues long and less than half a league wide which, along with another valley formed by a range, the fifth, rising on its west flank, has three missions,[5] eight Indian villages,[6] four active reales de minas,[7] two small settlements of Spaniards,[8] and an abandoned real.[9] These two valleys are more thickly populated, and their planted fields outnumber those of the Oposura Valley.

The fifth mountain range is about twenty leagues across and measures much less toward the south, narrowing more as it extends westward to Opodepe where it joins the sixth range.

The sixth range begins in the Pimería Alta, descends toward the south to Nacameri, where it is cut by the brook of that valley, and continues to San José de Gracia, Santa Rosalía, etc. Some of its ridges reach the mountain of Las Animas and almost join hands with the famous Cerro Prieto, running down its slopes to Guaymas near the Yaqui River. There are other ranges and hills farther to the west, but as they are much smaller than those described and the plains much larger, I find it advisable not to detail them. A long description would only exhaust the patience of the reader.

SECTION TWO
Fertility of the Soil

The upper and lower lands of the Pimas, as well as a portion of the land of the Eudebes, are not guarded by so many rugged mountains as are those of the Opatas, most of the Eudebes, and Jovas, though they

[5] Cumpas, Oposura, and Térapa.

[6] Teonadepa, Tamayoa, Técora, Toi-Serobabi, Tonibabi, Pivipa, Tepache, and Badéhuachi.

[7] Three of the reales were Todos Santos, Carrizal, and Carrizal de Abajo. The fourth one might have been either Basura or El Mortero.

[8] La Junta and El Salto.

[9] San Juan Bautista.

border some ranges. These latter lands are flatter, more extensive, and exposed to all winds. Ordinarily they are less fertile. The land of the Pimería Alta excels all others in this province. I recall having heard a righteous priest, an eyewitness, tell that from eight almudes[10] of corn, 500 fanegas had been harvested.

Although they reward well the labor of the worker, the returns in the rest of the province are not so great, rendering 25 to 50 fanegas from one of wheat and yielding 100 to 300 fanegas of corn from one fanega of seed.

Similarly, the lands of the Opatas and the Pimas give abundant returns of lentil beans and other legumes, but garbanzos, vetches,[11] peas, etc., do not come up to expectations except in a few areas. Beans, in some soils as those of Batuc, Mátape and Tecoripa, after two or three plantings, degenerate into a type that the natives call *tépari*.[12] It is of inferior quality, lesser in nourishment and smaller in size. The same thing happens with white cabbage. After two or three plantings, especially in warmer areas, it becomes a less desirable vegetable.[13] In colder climates, as in Bacerac, Cuquiárachi, Arizpe, and Pimería Alta, it retains its original quality longer.

[Note: The paragraphs that follow are not in the Mexico manuscript but were in the Smith text, Guiteras' translation.]

Sugarcane grows in most of the province, more abundantly in the hotter sections. Syrup is extracted from it and panocha[14] is made.

Sweet potatoes, carrots, turnips, radishes, lettuce, and whatever else grows in truck gardens might be sown and abundant yields obtained were it not for the scarcity of workers, for neither Indians nor whites are willing to apply themselves to such a task.

There are several varieties of pumpkins. One is called *camat* in

---

[10] A dry measure equal to half a bushel.

[11] Alberjas or chícharos. *Pisum sativum,* vetches.

[12] *Tépari* or *técari* is mentioned in Bolton's *Anza's California Expedition,* **4,** p. 99; also in Velarde's "Relación," p. 128.

[13] Nentvig makes no distinction between repollo, interpreted here as white cabbage, and col, presumably colored cabbage.

[14] Panochas are conical or rectangular dark-colored cakes made of the unrefined syrup.

Opata. It may be kept whole or peeled and cut into slices. If it is dried in the sun, it will keep for a year. Another is called *baborat.* It has a long neck and a hard rind. *Sosoc* is a small pumpkin that is harvested in the spring and eaten stewed or as salad.

Excellent melons and watermelons known as *bisicamat* are grown in abundance where there is no scarcity of water. These require little or no cultivation.

Millet, called *sagui* in Opata, is sown in small quantities, and pinole[15] is made from its seeds. The Jovas have another variety they call *coguet,* which is *ex Mexicani tzoalli.*[16] It has seeds which are similar to those of quelites[17] but yellow in color. The Jovas first gather the leaves, then pick the seeds, which are prepared in the following manner: Six bushels of seed, or as much as desired, are placed in a palm-leaf basket and taken to the river where they are immersed in the running water. The grain is then beaten, usually by stomping with one foot, until the grain bursts and makes a frothy mixture as it combines with the water. The grain is then roasted and ground. The resulting flour when mixed with cold water makes a refreshing drink.

All the fruit trees of Spain could be grown here, particularly peaches, apricots, figs, pomegranates, and quinces. Apples, pears, and Castilian nuts do better in the colder regions. Bananas grow well in some places while sweet or sour oranges, lemons, and even citron do well in the whole province.

SECTION THREE

The Climate

The climate of Sonora is hot rather than temperate, particularly along the Gulf of California, and in the marshes formed by the overflow of

[15] A nutritious beverage made of finely ground parched grain mixed with water or milk and sometimes sweetened.

[16] A detailed description of this is found in Trens' *México de antaño,* page 108.

[17] Quelites is a familiar weed [*Chenopodium album* or *Amaranthus powelli*] commonly known as pigweed or pot greens. It is eaten by the people of Sonora either cooked or raw in salads. L. S. M. Curtin in *Healing Herbs,* page 168, claims that the Moors had this vegetable under the name *qligl,* and that it is similar to the Aztec *quilitl.*

the Colorado River and on the central and southwestern plateaus, except Onavas and Cumuripa where it is colder, although it never freezes. The central and southwestern plateau area includes the following:

a) the lands around the banks of the Río Grande from Oputo on the north to the Yaqui Valley on the south
b) along the Río Chico, the towns of Nuri and Movas
c) the Tacupeto Valley, including Arivechi, Pónida, and Sahuaripa
d) all the Oposura and Batuc valleys
e) the Sonora Valley around Opodepe and Ures
f) all of the Tecoripa Valley

With the coming of the rainy season, called quipatas, during January and February the cold at night is severe. The peaks of the Sierras remain covered with snow while on the plains at lower elevations it melts as soon as it falls except in Bacerac, Fronteras, Cuquiárachi, Terrenate, and Santa María Soamca. Father Ignacio Javier Keller, founder and missionary of Soamca for over 30 years, used to say that on St. John's Day[18] summer sets in at 11 o'clock before noon and lasts until three in the afternoon of the same day. His long stay at Soamca makes his statement authoritative.

Epidemics — Sonora does not have regional diseases. Smallpox, usually fatal, fortunately strikes infrequently. Sonora's climate in general is healthful, not only for Creoles[19] but for natives as well. It is not unusual to find individuals from faraway countries such as Germany and Spain, Gachupines,[20] or people from the central plateau of New Spain, Mexicans[21] and Poblanos[22] of 68, 77, or more years of age. Of the native-born Sonorans, there are several close to 100 years of age. The most deadly misfortune, which will be taken up later, has been the arrow of the Seri and the lance of the Apache, scourges which have existed for quite some time as can be proven by the burial records.

[18] June 24th.

[19] Full-blooded Spaniards born on the American Continent.

[20] Derisive nickname for Spaniards.

[21] People from Mexico City.

[22] People from Puebla.

Only the Pimería Alta has proven adverse to the health of strangers, but in my opinion the cause of the trouble is not the climate or the air but the impurity of the water, for all the streams come from swamps and flow through shady, wooded ravines. Perhaps they contain injurious substances either mineral or vegetable that come from the soil over which they flow. For this reason it would be well to experiment boiling and exposing the water to the night dew. Also a sprig of cinnamon or something else such as the root recommended by Father Gumilla[23] for this purpose might be added before boiling.

There is an ailment, almost regional, particularly among the Pimas, presumably affecting those from both the upper and lower regions, which they call *saguaidodo,* or yellow vomit,[24] that causes several deaths each year. For the treatment of the disease Father José Och[25] devised two remedies so efficacious that, as his reverence assured me, no one who took one or the other perished. On the contrary, all got well in two or three days.

The first treatment[26] consists of burning a handful of dry sage [estafiate], mixing the ashes in atole[27] and drinking it. The sage used is called *cupiso*[28] in Opata and not the other specie they call *túparo*[29] which has no known virtue except that of driving away bedbugs. The herb is spread under the mattress if one can stand the offensive odor.[30]

---

[23] Joseph Gumilla, S.J., author of *Orinoco ilustrado.*

[24] Very likely yellow fever.

[25] Father Och, S.J., a native of Franconia, Würzburg, Germany, was stationed in Sonora from 1756 to 1765. In his reports he mentions and describes the sickness mentioned here and also others not touched upon by Father Nentvig, such as measles, tuberculosis, and lues venerea. Cf. *Missionary in Sonora,* Treutlein's translation, 1965.

[26] The second treatment, not given in the Mexican manuscripts, consisted of dried, ground orange peeling dissolved in atole. *Ibid.,* page 171.

[27] A gruel made of boiled maize ground to a pulp and dissolved in water or milk.

[28] *Salvus,* a plant of the mint family.

[29] Wormwood.

[30] The good father may have confused the words. *Túparo* is considered to be *Artemisia absinthius,* known as a tonic and vermifuge; the odoriferous one is probably any one of the various mugwort *Artemisiai.*

Concerning the nations living along the Gila and Colorado rivers, the most convincing proof of the healthful qualities of the climate is found in the great numbers of people in the villages and their robust natures. According to accounts of priests who have visited them for the last sixty years, neither has decreased. The only decline noted is in their desire to become Christians. It is regrettable that for lack of missionaries so many thousands of souls have been and are being lost.

SECTION FOUR

Pertaining to Cattle and Their Breeding[31]

Mexico City is well aware that Sonora does not lack the capacity to raise all breeds of stock, as during peaceful epochs, large consignments were sent there from Mátape. The fame of our mules was well known there, although at present even in this province there is a shortage of cattle which includes cows, oxen, mules, and horses. The shortage is so acute that residents do not have enough beef to slaughter or saddle animals to ride in quest of sustenance for their families. The shortage should not be attributed to the climate because there is none better suited for breeding purposes, but to the prowling of the Apaches and the Seris. One needs only to look at the nearly 300 abandoned ranches and estancias that have lost more than 4,000 mules, mares, and horses in the last seven years to realize this is true. Not many years ago, a former governor of New Mexico drove a considerable number of mules of all brands[32] without the appropriate markings through Chihuahua. The stolen animals, even if found, are never returned to Sonora.

The truth is that many have been stripped of their animals by the enemy, and it is necessary for them, if they are desirous to start anew, to obtain stock from outside the province. The little that remained

[31] In Spanish, cattle (ganado) is a generic word applicable to all animals and subdivided into large (mayor), such as bovines, horses, mules and donkeys, and small (menor), such as sheep, goats, and hogs.

[32] This is Father Nentvig's first reference to the branding of cattle. It was customary for the seller to brand the animal a second time. Then the new owner would place his brand below this. The double-brand showed that the animal had been legally sold, and the brand below signified the new owner.

untouched by the thieves was at the Movas Mission, and even that has been claimed by the Seris and their allies, the Pimas, with the assistance of the Babarocos.[33]

Asses thrive and multiply in Sonora in spite of the frequent and repeated thefts by the Apaches, and because these animals maintain themselves on little and can find food in the refuse heaps of the settlements, those living in the province utilize them as the principal beasts of burden.

Sheep do not reproduce so well as cattle. One of the reasons for this, in my opinion, lies in the density and thorniness of the brambles in some places, for in more open terrain the sheep increase in number at a better rate. Another reason could be that the breeders never separate the rams from the ewes, and through the seasons, hot or cold, they mate twice yearly. Because of the strain of being pregnant and nursing at the same time, the ewes age rapidly, grow lean, wander off, and die early. For the same reason, not half or even a fourth of the young survive. Finally, because of the fear of enemy raids, the sheepfolds are kept within the village. If they were in suitable locations, no province could be better provided with sheep than Sonora.

SECTION FIVE

Wild Beasts Found in the Province

The quadruped called lion [cougar or mountain lion] here—*naidoguat* in Opata—is not the king of beasts he is in other countries. Almost as large as a yearling calf, this animal is so passive and cowardly that it does not fight when cornered but whines and cries instead. It is true that because of its size and strength it does damage and kills domestic animals, but it has neither the mane, color, nor claws of the real lion. Some call it leopard, also a misnomer.

The tiger [jaguar or ocelot], *tutzi* in Opata, found throughout the province, is fiercer and does more harm to beasts of burden and cattle than does the lion, but does not attack man unless cornered.

Another fierce and harmful animal is called *guaicuri* in Opata and resembles a bobcat. The Opatas call the wildcat *poro* [American lynx,

---

[33] Residents along the banks of the Babaroco River on the eastern slope of the Sierra Madre Occidental, county of Chínipas, state of Chihuahua.

Lynx rufus], a rather fierce animal that attacks one whose shot has failed to kill it.

Bears, which the Opatas call *mava,* are found in the higher mountains. And there is another variety which they call *pissini.*

Wolf in Opata is *teona*; coyote is *go*, and fox is *cao*. There seems to be a third species which is unnamed, a mixture of dog, wolf, and fox. Wolves attack the larger cattle, while coyotes and foxes prey on sheep and poultry.

The raccoon [*Nasua nasica*], *batepi* in Opata, does much damage, gathering ears of corn all night long and carrying them off to its burrow. A similar animal is the badger [*Procyon lotor*], *churei* in Opata, which does the same thing.

There are also deer, which the Opatas call *massot,* a kind of stag but only half the size. There is a larger animal of the same species we call bura,[34] and the Opatas call *xua.* These roam the plains of both Pimerías and the Seri country. The males grow antlers, those of the *massot* being much smaller than those of the bura. In the entrails of the deer, especially those of Seri land, one finds bezoar stones,[35] thought to be a coagulum caused by the great thirst they suffer on account of the scarcity of water. The bura has them also, but they are not held in such high esteem. The antlers when dried, broken into pieces, powdered or scraped, and applied to the skin act as an antidote for the bites of poisonous reptiles. [Broken into pieces, the antlers resembled rocks and were known as piedra de la ponzoña, poison stone, in Sonora.]

There are many wild pigs, called *mutza* in Opata, in the mountains, not so large as the European boar but as black and with less dense bristling. In all respects these are similar to the domestic hog except that the navel is up in the loin.[36] In order to use its meat, hunters must carry a reed or hollow cane to insert in the navel the

---

[34] Mule deer.

[35] Acosta in his *Historia natural y moral de las indias,* book **IV,** chapter 42, discusses bezoar stones and their use among the aborigines.

[36] In chapter 38 of *Historia* ... , Acosta reports that this animal has the anatomical deviation cited by Nentvig. Oviedo, in *De la natural historia de indias,* chapter xix, agrees. However, Clavijero in his *Historia antigua de México,* **II,** p. 204, explains that the odoriferous substance was secreted by a gland located in the middle of the back which was erroneously taken to be the navel. These animals are musk-hogs and were called *peccari* by the Opatas.

moment the pig falls dead, for this causes the vaporizing of the musk contained in this area. Otherwise, the musk taints all the flesh and no one can eat it regardless of how hungry one may be.

Many wild sheep [*Carneros cimarrones*], *teteso* in Opata, are found in the Pimería Alta; there are fewer in the rest of the province. These wild sheep are larger with longer and bulkier horns by far than the tame ones.

Wild goats,[37] called *cubida* by the Opatas, roam in herds in open country, and when not grazing they move one behind the other in single file regardless of their number, making a path so narrow that it is hardly wide enough for a man's foot.

Sonora has an abundance of hares, called *paro* in Opata, so many that a garbanzo field sown in October is devastated by winter. Unless they are continually driven off, the whole crop is lost. The way of hunting them or scaring them off is for the natives to form a line beyond the planted patch, the natives standing as close together as their numbers will allow. Then they advance toward the village making as much noise as possible and herding the hares out of the field. Often they are chased into the huts in the village. It is not a bad amusement.

There are more than a few rabbits, called *tabú* in Opata, but the Indians are not inclined to hunt them for food because they do not satisfy the appetite.

Squirrels, ardillas or arditas, *hore* in Opata, are so numerous that they often devastate some crops while the crops are still young and tender, such as garbanzos, vetches and the like, if these crops are located near the area where they have their burrows. There are also flying squirrels, called *Sciurus volucella* in Latin and *tusas* in Opata. They live in pine trees in the mountains.

There are three small animals similar in appearance to the squirrel with black and white markings and a bushy tail. They are called [skunks in English], zorillos in Spanish and *hupas* in Opata [zoologically they are *Mustelidos* of the genus *Mephitis americana*]. The animal is usually black with white stripes. Another type is called *vacahupa* in

[37] In Spanish, berrendos. They have a chestnut colored body and a white belly. Pfefferkorn's *Description of Sonora* refers to them as roe deer, which is also correct.

Opata and has a white tail. The third type is called *doriguino* by the Opatas. All three are pretty, but if anyone attracted by their beauty and tameness tries to capture them, for they do not run from those who approach them, they eject an offensive-smelling, musky liquid that scalds the skin and has such a stench that however often one may change his clothes and bathe, he will not rid himself of the penetrating odor. Time will gradually take the smell away.

SECTION SIX

Insects and Disgusting Creatures

There is no lack of small, fierce, red ants, *arit* in Opata. Their bite hurts more than the sting of the scorpion, *tomevego* in Opata, which is not deadly in Sonora although a few people have gotten lockjaw from its sting. If this occurs, it can be cured easily by taking the gum *jua,* with which we will deal later.

Black ants are plentiful in all the province and do much damage to gardens, for they cut the buds and tender sprouts as soon as they appear and carry them off to their anthills. The Opatas call them *mocho,* and the Spaniards call them mochomos.[38]

Sonora has three types of vipers: The rattlesnake [*Crotalus atrox*], *co* in Opata, the bite of which is fatal to man or beast unless it can be attended to immediately; the black-tailed snake [*Crotalus molossus*], *sadaco* in Opata; and the *teveco* [*Bothrops atrox*].[39] This last viper is feared more than the others because it strikes without warning when one is not even aware of its nearness.

The most common and efficacious remedy consists of securing the head of the snake between two sticks, keeping the head in such a position that the snake cannot bite. Then the tail is held firmly and stretched out so that the snake cannot coil. The victim of the snakebite then bites the snake. At this point something truly remarkable happens. The patient does not swell, but the snake does, monstrously so, until it bursts.

---

[38] The ant called mochomo in Spanish is actually dark red.

[39] This is probably the *vívora sorda* referred to by Pfefferkorn in *Description . . .*, p. 126, as "the silent snake."

Other treatments consist of burning the bitten spot with a hot iron or piercing it with a knife and applying powdered, parched antler. However, when none of these remedies work, a few swallows of human excrement dissolved in water are taken by the injured one whose love of life makes this imperative. Father José Och of the Society tells me of having experimented successfully with ginger. It is first chewed and mixed with saliva then applied to the wound.

There is a four-footed kind of lizard called escorpión [Gila Monster, *Heloderma suspectum*], *sacara* in Opata, which is very poisonous and has a stumpy tail and markings of various colors. It is claimed that there is no other cure for its bite than to cut away the affected part immediately. It runs fast after its prey and seems to draw its victim to it with its deadly breath, swallowing it whole as does the buyo [boa constrictor], according to Father Gumilla. Someone once told me he had seen an escorpión with half a rabbit in its mouth, having already swallowed the other half.

The Opatas speak of a large, bulky, dark-colored snake called *coro* [black king snake, *Lampropeltis nigritus*] which is harmless to humans but draws small animals and even deer with its breath and swallows them whole. They are excellent rat hunters; therefore the natives use them instead of cats.

Another snake, called *macapsino*[40] by the Opatas, is frequently found in roof tops. It is red and black and resembles the coral snake. They claim it is venomous. Also it is said that if it falls from any height it breaks into pieces.

The whip snake [*Masticophis flagelum*], called *setagui* by the Opatas, is a nonpoisonous reptile. However, it lashes with its tail, thus making the bare-legged Indian leap briskly when he accidentally treads upon one.

There are two other nonvenomous snakes: a spotted one called *vabome* and the *ovisonó*, which is dark-colored.

The centipede [genus of *Myriapoda*], *massiguat* in Opata, is so named because of its many legs. It is very poisonous, and when it attaches itself to a human part, the area becomes painful and turns

---

[40] This might be the glass snake, *Ophisaurus ventralis*, except that the *Ophisaurus ventralis* is harmless.

dark. The remedy is simple enough: pour hot water on the bitten part and rub up and down.

There is a large black spider with a few yellowish hairs on its back: the tarantula [*Lycosa* or *Mygale* tarantula], *mariguasoco* in Opata. Its sting is said to be fatal. Yet as many as there are here, I have not known of anyone who has died from its venom, although a soldier from the Fronteras presidio assured me that the steed he was riding, having stepped upon one, stopped suddenly. Upon looking for the cause, he found the trampled tarantula dead and his horse's hoof fallen off.

We have here a poisonous spider, the sting of which is deadly to children. It is called ubari in Spanish, *guitoc* in Opata [probably the black widow, *Lactrodectus mactans*]. The treatment for its sting consists of slicing the area, making it bleed, and applying poison stones[41] to draw the venom out, although the pain and itching persist. I was stung, and upon applying a stone, it jumped and broke in two.

There are other spiders that are harmless.

Bedbugs [*Cimex lectolaria*] are also found here and are called chinches de Compostela in Spanish. They are small, wingless, nocturnal parasites that sting. And their sting causes more suffering than does the bite of a scorpion because it is followed by a tormenting distress throughout the whole body. The pain is relieved by drinking Sonora gum[42] dissolved in warm water, but the burning sensation persists for many hours.

A larger black beetle, called pinacate [stink bug], *teura* in Opata, is found here. Its poisonous sting causes great pain, and what is worse, one cannot harm it or drive it away without great discomfort to one's sense of smell, for the beetle pollutes the atmosphere with its stench.

There are also cockroaches, crickets, and other vermin. Let what has been said be enough about disgusting creatures.

---

[41] Bezoar stones, especially from the entrails of a deer as mentioned in section five, were thought to have great curative powers. Nentvig uses the term piedra de la ponzoña when he refers to powdered antlers. The words mean stone of poison.

[42] Sonora gum, gomilla de Sonora, *Coursalia glandulosa,* is a transparent, reddish-yellow resin exuded by a bush called samota, *Heliocarpus attenuatos* or *Pouzolia nivea.* The bush is indigenous to southwest Sonora, and the exudate is the result of the action of the insect *Coccus lacca.*

SECTION SEVEN

The Birds

Let us enjoy the sweet songs and behold the harmonious varieties of the colorful plumage of the countless birds that fly through this air. Foremost, let us consider the double-headed eagle, *scipipiraigue* in Opata, which was seen in these lands long ago, according to tradition.[43] There are two other kinds of eagles, both with single heads. One is called *pague* by the Opatas, and the other is called *pichuchu*.

There is a large bird of the hawk family that is called *taguara* by the Opatas and a night-hunting bird they call *doquetaguara*.

There are three types of owls, [classified under the generic term of] *tecolote:*[44] one is called *muhu*[45] by the Opatas; another, the lechuza [*Strix passerina*], they call *nacamu,* and the third they call *teramut*.

Moreover, there is a bird called *guegue* [*Phainopepla nitus*] in Opata, guerrero in Spanish. It has a song which is taken as an omen of war. Because of its ominous portent, it is also known as *sumagua* [war bird or warrior].

More than a few domestic chickens are raised in Sonora, and in some sections there are ducks, turkeys, red-billed pigeons [*Columba flavirostris*], called *cui* in Opata; mourning doves [*Zenaidura macroura*], tórtolas in Spanish and *ococoi* in Opata; and mockingbirds, zenzontle in Spanish and *tzepa* in Opata, the bird with a hundred voices. There is also an abundance of quail of various kinds, some with tufts. There is one kind called coitzi, gambel or desert quail [*Lophortix gambelli*]. There is another known as *cocco* that has a larger tuft. [This is probably the Douglas quail, *Lophortix douglasii.*]

And there is a bird called *churu* by the Opata which the Spaniards call cardinal because its color and crest resemble the clothing and biretta of the empurpled princes of the Catholic Church.

---

[43] A specimen was sent to King Philip V in 1723, but one must assume it was a biological abnormality rather than a bird of a separate specie.

[44] This is from the Aztec *tecolotl*.

[45] The name is probably derived from the sound the bird makes. This is probably true of many of the other Opata names for birds as well.

Furthermore, wild turkeys [*Meleagris gallopava*] still exist in the extreme northeastern portion of Sonora and are called *chiqui* in Opata. There are also cranes, gray and white geese with black feathers in the wings, herons, ducks, and many other kinds of fowl, so many that it would require a whole lifetime to learn their names.

One I certainly do not wish to omit is the world's tiniest bird, the hummingbird, chuparosa in Spanish and *semu* in Opata [rose-sucker]. At first glance it appears to be a butterfly, but when one looks closely, one sees that it is a perfectly formed bird in full plumage. At one time it was believed that this bird bore its young *expultrix* as do humans. But now we know that it builds a nest, lays eggs, and hatches them as do all birds.

IV

Native Flora

SECTION ONE

Fruits

Pitahaya [*Cereus trigonis*],[1] *Ychivo* in Opata, is foremost among the wild fruits of Sonora, equally relished by Spaniards and gente de razón[2] as well as the aborigines. It is available from the latter part of May through June and July. It grows on a plant with thick, tall stalks similar to Paschal candles except that they are octagonal, green, and well provided with thorns not at all different from the quills of the hedgehog. It has no leaves or branches but off-shoots, one from another, decreasing in thickness proportionately and similar in structure to the one that serves as trunk. From the stalks or shoots, white or somewhat purplish flowers arise which wither in about fifteen days, and the developing bud, attached to the stalk without a stem, remains green until it reaches the size of a hen's egg, sometimes much larger. Then it turns dark red, a sign that the fruit is ripe. There is so much of this fruit that the natives gather it both for themselves and to sell. There are many ways to prepare it. Its sweet flavor is not disagreeable, even to outsiders.

The fruit itself is covered with spines, and to remove them requires the stolid, patient temperament of the natives. This done, the thin rind is opened. The thinner the rind, the more savory the fruit.

---

[1] Pitahaya is the fruit of the giant cactus, *Carnegiea gigantea*.

[2] Gente de razón literally means people of reason. In Nentvig's time it meant specifically anyone with white blood flowing through his veins, i.e., anyone not 100% Indian.

The inside is all meat interspersed with innumerable tiny seeds on the order of mustard, but the whole is edible.

The saguaro,[3] which I have seen only in the Pimería Alta, has a taller and thicker stalk than the plant which bears the pitahaya, but the fruits of these plants differ only in that the saguaro's is sweeter than the pitahaya.

Next in importance is the tuna [prickly pear], *nabú* in Opata, Indian fig in Spain. It is the fruit of the nopal [*Cactus opuntia*], *nacó* in Opata. This plant, as the preceding ones, grows wild but would do better if cultivated. Two crops are gathered from the nopal, the first during March and April. The tender sprouts, called nopalitos, are cut, boiled and dried. Because of their tartness, they are used as relish for pinole.[4] The second harvest is that of the fruit itself, the tuna, which when ripe is found in different sizes and colors.[5] Since the fruit is well known in Spain, I will omit is description. I do say that the tuna, because it brings on fevers, etc., is not so healthful as the pitahaya.[6]

Of the palm tree family, there is one called *sot* by the Opatas that bears fruit called dátiles weighing one or two pounds, but the trees do not grow everywhere.[7] Other species of fruit-bearing palms, generically called *tacos* and *tacut* in Opata, are of two types: the first has fruit about the size of a pigeon's egg. This fruit, called *viviso* in Opata, has a stone-like seed that is occasionally used in the making of buttons.

---

[3] Nentvig implies that this plant is different from the *Carnegiae gigantea* (note 1 above). It is not. It simply grew larger and was known by another name in the Pimería Alta.

[4] Pinole is finely ground, parched corn. The Guiteras version further adds that nopalitos are also used as relish for several kinds of meat and atole (a gruel made of Indian corn ground or pounded then boiled in water or milk). The Mexico manuscript does not include this.

[5] There are seventeen varieties, according to Santamaría's *Diccionario de Mejicanismos,* p. 1094. Two varieties prevail in Sonora: the *tuna de Castilla (Opuntia fiscus indica),* very light green or yellowish, and the *Opuntia engelmanni,* which is red or purple.

[6] The good father was misinformed. Both are healthful and nourishing.

[7] This is probably the coconut palm, cocotero in Spanish, *Cocos nucífera* in Latin.

And the other, known as *jovegue,* bears a better quality of fruit that is smaller.[8]

And not to be left out is the palmito [*palmetto,* fan palm]. The natives eat the center portion of the trunk. First they strip away the palm leaves. From these they make mats called petates, *hipet* in Opata. Then they clear away the layer of shag which is found matted among the fronds, and after peeling the hard and horny covering off the trunk, they reach the edible part that weighs as much as twenty-five pounds. This, raw or warmed over a fire, provides food for four or six people. It is said that it tastes like coconut, something I cannot confirm because I have not eaten any.

The mezcal, *vitzo* in Opata, is an agave [century plant] similar to maguey [*Agave atrovirens*] but smaller, having flat, wide, long, pointed leaves, each armed with a sharp spine at the top. From the leaves stripped of pulp muleteers obtain a very good fiber called pita [agave fiber, hemp] that is known as pita de España in Europe. Leaves sprout out of the stalk. And poor folk get food in times of scarcity by roasting the stalk. Ordinarily it is the nourishment of those who are little inclined to work.

By roasting and mashing the stalk, then placing it in water which is brought to a boil, a very good liquor is made. Some have attempted to give this liquor a bad reputation by saying it is injurious to the health of humans, but I as an eyewitness can truthfully testify that there are individuals nearly one hundred years old who I know favor a swallow of it now and then. Therefore, I have reached the conclusion that its moderate use causes no harm. As it is with all strong drink, it is imbibing in excess that is a vice. I make this assertion because I wish to establish the truth. This liquor, when applied externally to wounds or bruises caused by blows or falls, is very efficacious. There are a thousand other uses. The virtues of it are too many to enumerate. Of this plant, the buds, commonly called quiotes[9] in Sonora and *varet* in Opata, as well as the buds of the palmilla [*Yucca elata,* soap-tree yucca], *corogue* in Opata, are edible when roasted. When in season these and sugarcane [*Sacharum officinarum*],

[8] This is probably the date palm.

[9] Quiote is the center portion from which the leaf-like blades sprout.

which is sucked,[10] are the only provisions that the natives carry on their journeys.

There is another plant resembling the palmilla. Although the top is as large, the spread of its leaves is much smaller. It is called lechuguilla, *cu* in Opata.[11] It has the same uses and effects as the palmilla when it is processed the same way. As for eating, the lechuguilla has more meat and is sweeter but somewhat biting.

The *maqui*[12] belongs in this group and provides the everyday bread for the Jovas. Its roots resemble those of the sweet potato [camote or batata]. Its skin is grayish, but the meat is white. While very poisonous if eaten raw,[13] causing death to the partaker, if it is boiled two or three times, each time in different water until it ceases to froth, it can be eaten safely. This is similar to the cassava of Puerto Rico, Campeche, and Cuba, except that the maqui is less coarse or woody. After the two or three boilings it is pounded and boiled again until a sort of dough settles at the bottom. This mass is then kneaded into loaves, tamales, or tortillas and cooked on cajetes.[14] It is the daily bread of these Indians, and they prefer it in spite of their having abundant crops of maize, wheat, and other grains. The leaves of this plant are large and divided like the fingers of a hand, and the lance-like sections, with spines at the sides, are also used. After being mashed by pounding, the mass is left to rot a little. Then it is spread upon mats, dried in the sun, and stored for future use, at which time the mass is boiled again and eaten with pinole.

The same use is made of *temaqui*,[15] the white root similar to the

---

[10] Sugarcane has to be chewed in order to squeeze out the juice.

[11] This is possibly either *Agave lechuguilla* or *Agave teteracanthae*.

[12] Possibly *Yucca manihote dulcis*.

[13] According to "La Relación de Sahuaripa de 1778" by R. H. Barlow in *Memorias de la Academia Mexicana de la historia* **VI,** no. 1, (1947): 76, the partaker swells up and dies immediately.

[14] Cajete, at present commonly known as comal, is a flattened, bowl-like utensil about twenty inches in diameter made of unburnished clay.

[15] Pfefferkorn calls *temaqui* wild sweet potato and describes it as being reddish with an unpleasant flavor (*Description of Sonora*, p. 55). Barlow's "La Relación de Sahuaripa de 1778", pp. 75–6, adds that it is an efficacious antidote for the poisoned arrow wounds of the Seri.

root of parsley but not so straight. The plant reaches the size of clover, but its leaves are more fissured and drooping. It puts forth a yellow flower during April. The natives eat this flower as a delicacy or just for fun as they do the fruit called toviri which is like a small, half-grown peach. The root is wholesome food without the danger of maqui for Indians as well as for destitute and impoverished Spaniards. Tortillas, atole, and pozole[16] are made of *temaqui,* and those who use it claim it is good for stews. Thus, the land of Sonora provides for its residents abundantly, even for those who have not the mettle to till its soil.

The mezquite tree [*Prosopis juliflora*], *quiot* in Opata, is found throughout the hot and temperate regions of the province. The natives harvest these trees twice a year, the first being in April when the pods are tender. They are boiled and dried for later use in their stews. The second harvest is in June when the pods, called péchitas, have ripened. Some are eaten at the time of picking, but the greater portion is saved to make atole and other dishes. The mezquite gives off an edible gum, *quio-chucat* in Opata, similar to the gum or jelly of Michoacán. It also gives off *quio-possore,* a sap employed in the treatment of sores. *Quio-possore* is used in place of blue vitriol.

On the crags of mountains, canyons, and ravines a good-sized tree grows that thrusts its roots into the rocky fissures. Its bark is yellowish while the leaves resemble those of the poplar[17] but longer. Its fruit looks and tastes like the common fig. Both fruit and tree are called *sassata.* Some believe this tree to be the suelda-consuelda [comfrey, either *Chroccoca alba* or *Symphytum officinali*] or the tescalama

---

[16] According to Pfefferkorn's *Description* . . . , p. 195, pozole as it was prepared by the missionaries for the Indians consisted of husked corn, wheat, peas, beans, and fresh or salted meat cooked together in a large kettle. Today it is made by boiling maize in lime water until the kernels burst and become soft (hominy). To this are added beans, which have been cooked for two or three hours, and any kind of meat. The mixture is then salted and spiced with chili.

[17] The leaves of the poplar are heart, ovate, or lozenge shaped while those of the common fig are lobed. Perhaps Nentvig had in mind the wild fig, *Ficus labrate.* Some species have edible fruit, elongated leaves and exude a rubber-like, milky sap.

[*Ficus potislaris*]. If a young petiole is broken, it exudes a milky fluid so effective as a medicine that I have seen contusions and fractures healed with it. Once a crazed cow attacked an Indian, crushing his clavicle and badly bruising the tissue. Almost dead, he was taken home on a litter, but following the application of this remedy he recovered so completely that he, who I thought would remain crippled for life, returned to his job as baker at the Huásabas Mission[18] and is still there.

The garambullo, *güero* in Opata, is a small cactus [*Cereus garambullo*] that does not have the edible center of the agave. It blooms from April to June, and its fruit is used as a febrifuge.

The wild grape [*Ampelocissus acapulcensis*] grows in damp ravines, climbing over willow, poplar, and mesquite trees. In Spanish it is known as uva silvestre, in Opata, *huragüe*. It bears a small, reddish-yellow fruit which ripens in May and June, long before the cultivated varieties, and is about the size of a garbanzo or alberjón.[19] Although they contain little nourishment, both the fruit and the leaves are eaten by the natives. The fruit is quite acid and occasionally is used to make vinegar and even wine.

The Mexican elder [*Sambucus mexicana*] is a fairly common tree in both Pimerías. From its berries the Altos make a beverage so potent that those who drink it to excess get so drunk that it takes two or three days to sober up. Believing that such vice is the cause of many evils, the missionaries have tried unsuccessfully to stop the Indians from making it.

The uvalama [*Vitex mollis*],[20] *sobaro* in Opata, is an uncultivated, rather large tree with luxurious foliage that grows in the warmest districts. Its leaves resemble those of the fennel [hinojo, *Foeniculum vulgare*] though larger and thicker. Its fruit, about the size of a large olive but not elongated, is also called uvalama and has a somewhat disagreeable taste. The fruit ripens in September.

---

[18] Nentvig was stationed at Huásabas from 1762 to 1767.

[19] Chickling vetch, *Lathyrus sativa*.

[20] It is indigenous to Mexico and unknown in the United States. The fruit, which is black, is boiled in water and sweetened with panocha (solidified sugarcane juice) to make it more appetizing. It is eaten with relish by the natives.

A more common fruit is the bebelama, *juco* in Opata. It is the size of a small olive and quite sweet. Although they are terribly hot, there seem to be no ill effects upon the stomachs of the natives who eat them in large quantities during May, the time when this fruit ripens. The tree from which it comes [*Bumelia laetevirens*] is of medium size and has small, tongue-shaped leaves.

The sapuche, *tesavo* in Opata, is a fruit that belongs with the others I have mentioned. It comes from a small tree about a yard in height with a slender trunk, and the leaves as well as the fruit resemble those of the pear tree [*Pyrus communis*].[21]

Acorns grow in the colder sections. Known to the Opatas as *cusit,* they are a desirable food for sturdy stomachs. I have known a trader who dealt in acorns, which were not the least important item in his inventory of merchandise. He sold them in the gold placers and mining camps.

The bachata [oak nut], *batzat* in Opata, is a small, dark-colored fruit the size of a garbanzo. It is very sweet, ripens in May and grows on a small bush not very different from the garambullo. Its roots serve the Indians as soap.[22]

Tlalayote [*Funastrum pannosum*], *tzoris* in Opata, is the name given to a small plant as well as its fruit which is about the size of a hen's egg and has a rough, coarse rind on the order of the shell of a snail. It must be eaten in the latter part of August when the skin is green and tender. Otherwise it hardens and dries, and the meat becomes soft, white and cottony as the meat of peyote.[23] The root of the tlalayote is poisonous to animals as are the roots of the yerba de Puebla [*chochoya, Senecio canicida*] and the babatoviri [yerba de la mora, *Croton cortesianus*]. All three are found throughout the province. The yerba de Puebla is an

---

[21] Barlow's "La Relación ...," p. 72 describes the fruit as small, resembling a mameyito *(sauravia serrate* or *Lucuma pedunculata).* At present, *sapuche* or *sapuchi* is the name given to zapote prieto *(Dyospiros ebenaster).* The fruit is similar to a pear in both size and shape, and the tree is 60 feet or more in height.

[22] There are several plants whose roots substitute for soap, but none has edible fruit.

[23] The Mexico City manuscript reads "peyote," very likely a copyist's error. It perhaps should read "pochote" *(Ceiba pentandra).* Pochote contains a substance used to make wicks for candles.

item found on all requisitions to Mexico City which shows the lack of curiosity on the part of the commissaries.

Nor are the mulberry trees [*Morus nigra*], *babiro* in Opata, lacking in Sonora. The wood is used for bows by the archers. But no notice is taken of the leaves which are utilized in other provinces. The berries, which are small, ripen in June and are very tasty.

The cúmaro[24] is a very large tree that abounds in Sonora. Its small fruit resembles that of the garambullo and is very sweet.

The madrone [*Arbutus texana*], *curibitso* in Opata, grows well in the mountains. In October its fruit ripens and is edible although at times it causes nausea and vomiting.

The wild manzanilla[25] is a small tree, the kind commonly known as chaparros [dwarfed]. The grape-size fruit is red and ripens in September. The Opata call both the plant and fruit *yori,* a Yaqui word meaning white people or non-Yaqui.

The Opata name *guetzat,* espino in Spanish, meaning thorn or needle, is given to a rather small, thorny tree[26] that bears red, sweet, garbanzo-size berries that ripen in June.

There are many other fruits which please and satisfy the people of Sonora. When they are away, they talk of them constantly. One could write an extensive treatise on the various wild herbs being used as food, but, as the subject is common knowledge here, I will end this section and begin the next, which deals with remedies employed to cure other ailments.

SECTION TWO

Medicinal Products

The providence of nature or should I say the Divine Providence?, has endowed Sonora, devoid of physicians, surgeons, and apothecaries, with excellent medicinal herbs, shrubs, gums, fruits, mineral and

[24] This could be the cohune palm *(Orbignya attalea cohune).* The fruit is called coquito de Colima. It resembles a coconut, being about two inches long, and is eaten mainly by cattle. Its seeds are eaten by the Indians.

[25] The tree described here appears to be the wild apple, manzanita silvestre in Spanish, *(Malvaviscus drummonddi)* which is plentiful in the province.

[26] This is probably graythorn or bluewood.

animal products of such quality that there is no collection like it in Europe. Besides the many herbs already known to medical science, here are others that are found in this province:[27]

acederas—sorrel leaves in salad
ajenjo—estafiate, or túparo—wormwood *(Artemisa mexicana)*
ajo—garlic *(Allium sativum)*
anís—anise *(Pimpinella anisum)*
apio—celery *(Apium sativum)*
azahar—orange blossoms

batatas—potatoes
bledo—wild amaranth *(Amaranthum blitum)*
borraja—borage *(Borago officinalis)*

cacahuates—peanuts
camotes—sweet potatoes
caña dulce or caña de azúcar—sugarcane
cardosanto or chicalote—blessed thistle *(Argemone mexicana, Cardus benedictus)*
cebadilla or eléboro—caustic barley, hellebore or sneeze-wort
cebolla albarrana—squill *(Scilla marítima)*
chicuri silvestre—wild chicory
cícuta—hemlock *(Conium maculatum)*
cominos—cumin
culantrillo de pozo—maidenhair fern *(Conuim maculatum)*
culantro—coriander *(Coriandum sativum)*

doradilla or citerach—a fern *(Sellaginella lepidophylla)*

endibia—endive *(Cichorium endivia)*
escarola—succory

fárfara or uña de caballo—colt's foot *(Tussilago farfara)*

grama—cynodon *(Capriela dactylon)*
granadas—pomegranates *(Punica granatum)*

[27] Nentvig presents the list grouped together within a paragraph. The list as tabulated here has the English equivalent followed by the botanical name as explained in the Preface.

hierba or yerba de la golondrina — swallow-wort *(Euphorbia maculata)*
higuerilla — castor oil plant *(Ricinus communis)*
hinojo — fennel *(Foeniculum vulgare)*

laurel — laurel *(Litsea glaucesens* and *Laurus nobilis)*
lengua de buey — marihuana *(Cannabis indica)*
limón — lemon
llantén — plantain *(Plantago)*

madroño — madrone *(Gomphrena decumbens* and *G. globosa)*
malva — mallow *(Malva rotundifolia)*
manzanilla — chamomile *(Helenium mexicana)*
mora or moral — mulberry fruit or mulberry plant *(Morus nigra)*
mostaza — mustard *(Sinapis nigra)*

naranja, dulce or agria — oranges, sweet or sour
nabos — turnips *(Brassica napus)*

olivo — olive tree
orégano — oregano or wild marjoram *(Origanum vulgare)*
ortiga — nettle *(Ortica dioica)*

peonía — peony *(Cyperus esculentos, Abrus precatorius)*
perejil — parsley *(Petroselinum sativum)*
pimiento — cayenne pepper, red pepper *(Capsicum)*
pimpinela — pimpinel *(Poterium sanguiserba)*
poleo — pennyroyal *(Clinopodium laevigatum* and *Menthae pulegeum)*

quelites[28] — pigweed, greens *(Amaranthus spinosum)*

rábanos — radishes
romero — rosemary *(Rosemarinus, Cowania mexicanae)*
rosa de Castilla — Castilian rose *(Lippia umbellata* and *Rosa centifolia)*
ruda — rue, ruta *(Prosela citriodora, Ruta graveolens)*

---

[28] Quelites is an article of food little known to nonresidents of Arizona, New Mexico, Texas, or Sonora. The people of New Mexico eat its oblong leaves as greens and call this vegetable pigweed. In Sonora it is eaten raw as greens in salads, but mostly the whole leaves of the *Chenopodium album* variety are cooked. The name is derived from the Aztec *quilitl*. There are several varieties.

salvia — sage (*Hyptis* species)
sangre de grado or sangre de drago — dragon's blood *(Jatropa dioica)*
sauco — elder *(Sambucus, Cerulea)*
siempreviva — house leek *(Selaginella lepidophylla)*
suelda-consuelda — comfrey *(Chroccoca alba)*
tomate, jitomate — tomato *(Lycopersicum esculentum)*
tomatillo or bainoro — garambullo (*Cereus garambullo,* an agave)
trébol — clover *(Trifolio)*
trementina — turpentine *(Therebintinus)*
verbena — vervain *(Verbena officinalis)*
verdolaga — purslane or watercress *(Portulaca oleracea)*
visco, toxi, or tzavo, also secapalo, cabellera, or injerto — mistletoe, a parasitic evergreen *(Phoradendron vernicusum)*
xarilla or jarilla — a resinous plant, terebintaceo *(Zaccagnia punctata)*
xicamilla or jicamilla — croton weed (*Jatropha macrorhyza,* a purgative)

One finds alum, copperas, bezoar stone, gypsum, sodium carbonate, saltpeter, and many members of the vegetable realm, including the sensitive plant,[29] but these are omitted so as not to weary the reader.

However, I do feel bound to include briefly the medicinal products which have virtues that seem to be unknown in other countries. These products have been discovered by the Indians and the old Spanish women who have set themselves up as a sort of royal tribunal of medicine.

The first is the anise herb, so-called by the Spaniards because its root tastes somewhat like anise [*Pimpinella anisum*]. The Opatas call it *guamusi.* The foliage resembles willow twigs, but only the root is used. It is taken internally by chewing, and swallowing the saliva. This aids digestion and eases discomfort caused by overeating and constipation. It also relieves stomachaches and the fever which often accompanies them.

[29] This is *Mimosa pudica.* The leaflets and stalks fold at the slightest touch or sound, such as the clapping of hands. The plant is quite prevalent in the region of the Panama Canal.

Next is the fever herb [*Iresine calea* of the *Amaranthus* family], *toninagua* in Opata, so named because of its ability to stop fevers unfailingly. A decoction is taken internally for a few successive days. Thus, without the expense of either doctors or drugs, the condition is relieved.

The rattlesnake weed [*Myriadenus tetraphyllus* or *Zornia tetraphrilla*], *conaguat* in Opata, is effective against snakebite. When a decoction is taken internally, it causes profuse perspiring and decreases a fever. This I have been told, but I have not been able to verify its effectiveness personally.

The spasm herb,[30] *paroqui* in Opata, when fried in oil or tallow and applied hot on the affected area, decreases inflammation and relieves tenseness of the muscles. When internal spasms are suspected in parturient women or individuals afflicted with other ailments, its decoction brings about good results. Even to beasts of burden, whether prostrate or spastic, a decoction is forcibly administered. The animals get well in a few minutes, take up their loads and resume the journey as if nothing had happened.

The herb of manzo grass [*Anemopsis californica*], *guaguat* in Opata, is decocted and used as a mouthwash to relieve the pain of toothaches. If taken internally, it allays the distress caused by certain maladies. Fried in tallow, it makes an ointment which when applied to fresh wounds or postpartum tears brings about healing. Equal results are obtained if the fried and powdered herb is used.

The swallow's herb [*Euphorbia prostrata*], *cozape* in Opata, has curative powers when decocted and applied to freshly inflicted wounds. The same results may be obtained by using the entire plant either dried or pulverized.

The decoction of the root of pipichagui, *taraigo* in Opata [probably *Perezia adnata*], a sort of wild lettuce, is a useful laxative. If taken internally, it relieves stomachache, griping, and amenorrhea. For this last it is a sure remedy if drunk once or twice even if the flow has been absent for three or four months. This condition is brought about because women are in the habit of bathing in the rivers regardless of

[30] Seep willow, yerba del pasmo in Spanish, is used to relieve symptoms of tetanus, lockjaw, and the common cold (coughing, sneezing).

the time of month. Even if it means certain death, when these creatures are ailing they keep silent about it until a missionary, called to hear confession, asks them about the nature of their illness. He then prescribes the cha.[31]

The decoction of the plant guanenepili, *vivinaro* in Opata [passion flower, *Passiflora tuberosa*], is an excellent cure for measles, smallpox, typhus, and contagious fevers. Continued use of the decoction after recuperation prevents the recurrence of the malady, thus lowering the risk of strain on the heart and other vital organs.

The cocolmecate is a plant that grows in mountains and rocky soils, putting out long creepers with red roots. If taken internally, the decoction made from these roots stops all pain and promotes menstruation. Its Opata name is *cocomeca* which actually means "away pain." [This plant is greenbriar, *Smilaxbona-nox*.]

The sánari, *ssan* in Opata, is a plant whose foliage and roots have astringent properties. The green leaves when applied to the anal region after defecation shrink hemorrhoids. Sánari, if roasted in an earthenware vessel then applied to a sore area, eases any pain. The decoction, if taken internally, acts as a violent and perilous cathartic. Those afflicted with syphilis who have tried other medications turn to sánari as a last resort. Occasionally they get well. [This could be *cuauhxiotl, Pseudosmodingium perniciosum*.]

The toloache [stinkweed, *Datura stramonium*], called *taguaro* in Opata, and the estafiate [sagebrush, *Artemisia mexicana*] are excellent remedies for tumors and abscesses because they bring them to a head. Those having spleen trouble obtain relief simply by rubbing a leaf upon the painful area every morning before breakfast.

The leaves of the chicura, *juguiro* in Opata, give relief to women who suffer from the hysteria which sometimes accompanies pregnancy. These leaves are warmed over hot ashes and applied to the abdomen. Equally effective is a tiny bit of gomilla dissolved and taken in warm water.

---

[31] Apocope of *pipichagui*. The root of this plant, when decocted and applied externally, Nentvig described as "para ayudas calientes," which may be interpreted as hot poultices applied around the chest and midsection since its principal function is the restoration of menstruation.

Sonoran gum, called *jua* by the natives, is the resinous exudate of a small tree commonly called *sámota* by the Opatas. Its aqueous decoction taken internally is an effective antivenom for the sting of scorpions, spiders, and other poisonous insects. It also relieves and prevents spastic seizures, allays anxiety, and slows down increased heart palpitations. I have witnessed some of its virtues and heard of many others, but as the gum has been accepted as a medicament by the Royal Tribunal of Medicine in Mexico City, to which goodly quantities are sent annually, I leave the subject to their scholarly presentation. [This is probably *Coursetia glandulosa*.]

The jojoba [*Simondsia californica*] is a well known shrub that grows in the Pimería Alta. Its fruit [goat's nut], also known as jojoba, is a treasure that the Indians always carry with them. If an Indian is wounded by an arrow, he will first remove the arrow then pack some nuts into the wound to prevent it from swelling until suction and treatment as described later can be instituted. Because the virtues of this fruit are well known in this realm, I am spared the enumeration of its marvelous curative properties. However, out of gratitude, I will not omit telling of the benefit I derived from its use shortly after arriving in this province. Having supped heartily on a good salad with vinegar, I suddenly felt violent pain in my left side under the lower ribs. I felt that I would suffocate, and I could scarcely speak to explain my predicament. The missionary father in whose house I was[32] brought two or three nuts, told me to eat them and gave me a cup of wine. No sooner had I eaten the jojobas and swallowed the wine than the intense pain disappeared.

The tepeguaje [*Lysiloma acapulcensis*], *matze* in Opata, is similar to, or perhaps actually is, the árbol del Perú [California pepper tree, *Schinus molle*]. Its bark boiled in water is an excellent antiseptic. When very dirty sores are washed with a concoction made from this, they stay clean and heal rapidly.

The cacalosuchil [temple flower, *Plumería acutifolia*], *caguirago* in Opata, is a shrub whose branches when broken or cut secrete a milky

---

[32] Father Nentvig arrived in New Spain on August 23, 1750, and was assigned to Sáric. It is assumed he was entertained by Father Campos at San Ignacio de Caburica.

sap which is beneficial to those afflicted with syphilis. Another herb named *tepuro* in Opata has the same curative properties. Moreover, a decoction of *tepuro* roots has anti-inflammatory qualities.

The hediondilla [creosote bush, *Larrea divaricata* or *Larrea tridentata,* gobernadora in Spanish], *cubiasisi* in Opata which means "roe deer's mane," has the same effects as cacalosuchil. An ointment is made by frying the fronds in tallow. A treatment which is said to be very efficacious for gnarled, rheumatic limbs consists of rubbing on the ointment and accompanying this with a suitable diet. It is claimed that if the masseur washes his hands after having applied the ointment his hands will become gnarled.

A priest of known integrity informed me that the decoction of damiana fronds [*Turnera diffusa* also *Trunera aphrodisiaca*], *tabuquit* in Opata, makes barren women fertile.

Cumeme is the name given by all Sonoran tribes to the skin of a root which when applied topically has strong caustic effects. It is used to relieve inflammation of the spleen and hasten drainage of tumors and abscesses.

The inmortal [immortal, desert milkweed, *Gomphrena decumbens*], *chupi* in Opata, *nitisi* in Apache, is an herb that grows in the coldest regions of Sonora. From its dried roots a powder similar to tobacco snuff is made which when sniffed alleviates headaches.

The ocosaguat is the name given to a pine tree. It is claimed that when its needles are burned in a room with a woman who is in the midst of childbirth, the fumes and healthful warmth induce easier delivery.

A similar claim is made of the *oquisegua,* an Opata word meaning "the blossoming of a woman," *flos mulieris* [probably *Vitex pyramidata* or *Salvia betónica*]. It also induces the menstrual flow.

Magot in Opata, yerba de la flecha in Spanish [arrow's herb of the spurge family, *Euphoria biloculare*], is a beautiful small tree with luxuriantly green foliage and deadly milky sap which was formerly used to poison arrows, hence the name. The milky juice is applied to stubborn abscesses to bring them to a head. Because of its poisonous nature, I would not recommend it.

Along the Guaymas coast grows the jaramatraca or caramatraca [*Wilcoxia tuberosus*], the tubers of which are an effective antitoxin for arrow poison. Father Francisco Pimentel, chaplain to the 1750 expedition against the Seris, assured me that if the wounded availed themselves of this remedy by chewing and swallowing it or by applying the chewed-up mass to the injury, no one died. This morsel is equally effective against flatulence. Moreover, it is also efficacious used as a poultice, pounded and mixed with firewater and applied to contusions, bruises, and open wounds. I am witness to its incredible and stupendous virtues. A cowboy who was trampled by a horse had his face mangled and some bones exposed. He was treated with this poultice, and his lacerations healed by the next day. Furthermore, individuals bitten by rabid animals do not develop hydrophobia if they take the ground root diluted in water. In addition, it is an efficacious antidote for poisonous snakebites, and it can cure typhus. As an ointment rubbed on an aching head, it brings relief and even stops toothaches. I have heard so much about the virtues of this root that if I were to give the title of panacea to any remedy, it would be this one.

Escoba amargosa [bitter broom, *Artemisa filifolia*], *sisicot* in Opata, romerillo in Spanish, is an herb that promotes healing of bone fractures, even those of the spine. A good handful of the herb is pounded, ground, and boiled in water. The brew is then stirred and skimmed until it assumes the consistency of a salve. In this form it is stored for future use. After a fractured bone has been set, the salve is spread upon the injured part, and unfailingly the bone mends.[33]

Sonora produces a universal medicament in the yerba del indio [Indian herb], trompetilla in Spanish and native dialects. Its tuberous root resembles the root of a sweet potato. When it is ground and dissolved in lukewarm water, many say that it is a remedy for fevers and all sorts of aches. Although extremely bitter, it can be chewed and swallowed. When pulverized and sprinkled in an open wound, it hastens healing. But it is seldom used because its application causes a great deal of pain.

---

[33] The salve hardens and serves as both splint and bandage. This cast-like dressing is allowed to remain in place for two months, ample time for the knitting of the fractured bones. Other plants that are purported to have the same qualities are the valley cottonwood (álamo de hoja redonda), the thistle (cardo santo, *Cardus tenniflorus*), the dandelion (chicoria, *Taraxacum officinale*), and the comfrey (suelda-consuelda, *Chroccoca*).

Uña de gato [cat's claw, *Acacia greggii,* less frequently classified as *Lantana camara*], *jussi* in Opata, is a shrub with short branches and curved thorns, hence its name. Its roots, long, slender and whitish, soaked in water, stirred and strained, will give prompt relief when there is urinary retention.

Calancapate [possibly *Senecio vulneraria*], *capoca* in Opata, is a sort of estafiate [*Artemisa mexicana*]. The decoction of its roots and foliage relieves stomachache. Furthermore, the natives use the fronds as pads, placing them under the saddles of their mounts in the belief that when the mount tires, fresh capoca will make the weariness disappear. Because of the abundance of the shrub in the province, there is never a problem of replacing the pad.

The *terachico,* known only by its Opata name, is a small tree. The natives dry the leaves and grind them into a powder which is used to cure sores of horses and other animals. Its roots when similarly prepared are employed in the treatment of human ulcerations [unidentifiable].

Also, the roots of mezquitillo [*Kameria paucifolia*], *temitzo* in Opata, and carrizo [bamboo, *Bambusa vulgaris*] are burned and pulverized and used to treat human sores.

Naguat[34] is a plant whose roots are said to be beneficial in the treatment of syphilis. They are beaten to a pulp and boiled in water. Then this mixture is drunk before breakfast.

The negrilla, known as *teah* to the Opatas, is used as an emmenagogue after delivery [unidentifiable].

In the Upper Pimería there is a creeping plant which has a root known as contrahierba [caltrop, contrayerba, *Dorstenia contrajerba*] that has the same virtues as the preceding. In addition, it relieves colds and intermittent fevers. Grated and added to lukewarm white wine, it is drunk when the chills begin. Then the patient drinks warm water. Vomiting ensues, and with that, the natives believe, the ailment disappears. It is also a well-known antidote for snake bites, stings of scorpions and other poisonous insects, but fearing that I might bore the reader, I will omit its many other properties.

---

[34] Probably this is either naguapacle from the Aztec *nanahuatl,* a bubo medicine, or creeping barberry, *Berberia repens,* a native blood purifier.

To attempt to name and describe all the medicinal plants that Sonora so lavishly produces would be an enormous task. If ten people were afflicted with the same ailment, each could use a different medication to effect a cure. Among the great variety of plants found in this province, there is hardly one without healing properties, while only a few are harmful.

As a corollary to this chapter, I must add some information about the treasure found in the mountains near Bacadéhuachi: a rock-salt which the natives pulverize and mix with tallow. The mixture is an effective cure when rubbed on a sore belly. If taken internally either as table salt as the Indians are prone to do, or diluted in water, it acts as a strong purgative.[35]

And finally, as a respite from the fatigue that this long dissertation may have caused, allow me to tell of a fragrant product of a worm. The worm, similar to a silkworm but differing in its abode, lives in either cold or warm regions. It clings to the rocky crevices of some of the mountains and weaves a cocoon called remolino de bola [whorl] in Spanish and *hecaguita* in Opata. This cocoon contains an aromatic, medicinal incense, the fumes of which when inhaled will cure malaria. As for the worm, upon completion of its work, it emerges from the cocoon and falls dead as does the silk-producing one. This is a salutary reminder to idle people of what the Holy Scriptures say: "that man was born to work" and "those unwilling to labor should be ashamed to eat,"[36] as I should be ashamed to be exhausting the patience of the reader.

---

[35] Undoubtedly this is magnesium sulfate of which Obregón in *Descubrimientos . . .*, p. 46, writes. And Pfefferkorn in *Description . . .*, p. 84, describes it as snow-white salt with a bitter taste and strong purgative effects.

[36] The first Biblical quote, i.e., "that man was born to work," is from the Book of Job, chapter v, verse 7, and the second, "those unwilling to labor should be ashamed to eat," is from the Second Letter of Paul to the Thessalonians, chapter iii, verse 10.

V

Indian Tribes of Sonora

SECTION ONE

Their Language, Nature, Intellectual Capacity, and Distinctive Traits

In the New World it is understood that groups of rancherías and villages that speak the same language form a separate nation. Thus in Sonora there are only two main nations: the Opata and the Pima. The Eudebes use a dialect as similar to the Opata language as Portuguese is to Castilian or Provençal is to French. And the Jovas are so intermingled with the Opatas that most of them speak in that language except a few women and old people who cling to their own, a most difficult tongue and very different from those spoken in this province.

The Upper and Lower Pimas speak the Piman language as do the Papagos who inhabit the sandy, barren plains of the northwest, the other tribes in the fertile valleys of the Sobahipuris, and those around the Gila and the Colorado rivers. According to Fathers Kino and Sedelmayr the dialects of these tribes differ, but their language is so similar that knowing one, it is easy to understand the others.

The Guaymas speak the language of the Seris with only a slight difference. Because some have surrendered their land to the bloody fury of the Seris and others have intermingled with the Yaquis in Belem and other places, the Guaymas being so few in number do not merit being classified as a separate nation.

As for the Seris and Apaches, the cruelest enemies and ravagers of the land, holding as their own the mountainous regions of this province, I do not deem it reasonable to include them in this section and will deal with them separately.

Their Nature — In general the nature of the native is so variable that it is hard to explain. My opinion, based on thirteen years of dealing with them, is in accord with Father Gumilla as stated in his *Orinoco ilustrado,* Part I, Chapter V, Section 5.[1] Their nature is based upon four traits, each more despicable than the one that follows: ignorance, ingratitude, inconstancy, and laziness. Their lives revolve around these peculiarities.

Their ignorance compels one to treat them as children regardless of their gray hair, which in them appears quite late.

As for ingratitude, one must do good solely for the sake of the Almighty, expecting no signs of gratitude from the natives and clothing himself with the firm belief that he is going to lose principal as well as interest.

Their inconstancy keeps the missionaries as well as civil and military authorities on continual watch, especially over the recently converted. A single malcontent or puffed-up egotist with a sorcerer's reputation such as Luis de Sáric is enough to stir up an entire nation. To this day we bewail the sad consequences of the insurrection of 1751 when the Pimas joined with the unrestrained Seris. This alliance still keeps the royal forces on the move.

Their laziness and horror of all work is such that neither exhortations nor pleadings nor even threats of punishment make them till the land to obtain their sustenance. This peculiarity keeps the natives poor and dependent upon the missionaries for their food and clothing. These items must be provided the year around to prevent them from wandering to mining camps where they will rapidly learn vices and forget their Christian teachings which have been taught to them over long years of inconceivable effort. The worst is that those who taste the licentious life seldom return to their villages. If they do, they become the devil's own leaven, teaching the wickedness they have learned and inciting many to abandon their wives and children for a

---

[1] Father Gumilla states: "Generally speaking, the Indian is definitely a man so uncivilized that I dare say he is a never-seen monster with a wild brain, an ungrateful heart, an inconstant soul, a lazy backbone, leaden feet, and a thirsty belly. And he is inclined to imbibe until drunk. All these things transform him, in a moral sense, into an irrational being." [Free translation.]

year or two which is a public offense to God our Lord. These runaways, sheltered by their employers, go on working on distant ranches a number of years and living with abducted women. Prodded by an awareness that they have done wrong, they are always on the alert so as not to be caught. They change places of employment frequently and their names as well. It is useless for the missionaries to send for the fugitives because the messengers return discontented and discouraged by the bad receptions and rebuffs handed them.

The inquiring reader may ask how can one reconcile the aborigine's innate attachment to the place of his birth, apparently so great that he will prefer to die rather than submit to being moved to improve his lot, with his voluntary exile? And how can we reconcile his reluctance to work, neighboring on fear, with the servitude he imposes upon himself? And if his ignorance borders on stupidity, how is it that he is astute and cautious enough to avoid being caught?

I can throw some light on these questions by stating that at the first farm, mining camp, or Spanish settlement they go to they will find instructors who in a couple of hours teach them the way into error, and the irreparable ruin of body and soul follows. Thus, the attraction of the detestable licentious life keeps them away from home where they enjoyed ownership of land and personal liberty and where they were subjected to only the easy duties of Christian living. The wife and relatives of the fugitive, knowing of his escape, never notify either the missionary or the magistrate, and when questioned they refuse to tell even the direction the runaway went, regardless of any offer of worldly goods and promise of secrecy. Here again is an evident contradiction in their nature, protecting one another by fiercely retaining a secret in spite of their inconstancy and fickleness.

In view of the many contradictions, one must confess that these Indians with their customs and inclinations are the opposite of others for, notwithstanding their uncultured state, they have the power to reason. To this is added our continual teaching, so that little by little the prickly briers are being uprooted and a political commonwealth, even a Christian one, will arise.

This, thanks to the Lord, we have accomplished chiefly with the Opatas and Eudebes who are more inclined to till the soil and breed cattle. Moreover, they are most attentive to their obligations at home. Consequently, they are the best instructed in the mysteries of our

Holy Faith. It has taken an unbelievable amount of work and zeal to make the natives do away with their usual phrase which was doubtless invented by the enemy of the human race: *sepore ma denit hui*[2] which they apply to anything not seen with their own eyes. Until the missionary succeeds in banishing this belief, the neophytes will never attain the faith required to accept the infallibility of God's authority and that of His Church.

SECTION TWO

Their History, Idolatry, and Sorcery

None of these nations has an alphabet, nor do they have any inclination to acquire one. Only a few ever learn to read and write, and in this respect I must acknowledge that the Apache children are better disposed. The natives in their ignorance and distrust fear that such art might be harmful to them. Thus, without even the simplest forms of writing, without even strings of beads or tallies which after a fashion were equivalent to writing to the Mexicans, Peruvians, and other nations, the Sonoran tribes have no record of their past except the confused and inaccurate accounts which have been transmitted from father to son. One can learn little from these. The Indian will relate only what he has seen and would give away his soul rather than reveal any secrets. He seems to be applying the Biblical quotation of Isaiah IV:16: *secretum meum mihi*.[3] Their own ridiculous explanations of the great religious mysteries are like the stories of children upon finding a bird's nest.

One might suspect from my last remark that I am implying that the natives are descendants of Jews. I am not. I do not agree with Scobar *(ut Scobar hic)*[4] [as Escobar states here].

The Sonoran tribes, including the Seri and Apache, have not been, nor are they now, nor have they a tendency to be, idolaters.

---

[2] "Perhaps thou speakest the truth."

[3] "The secret will remain with me."

[4] Perhaps Nentvig refers to the famed Spanish theologian Antonio Escobar y Mendoza, 1589–1669. In Yucatán at the time of the conquest he observed a ceremony in which the prepuces of children were pierced. He mistakenly thought this was the Hebraic ritual of circumcision.

There is not a trace of such worship, nor has any idol or other device been found to indicate such adoration.[5] The only homage noticed is to the devil, and this is based on fear and stupidity rather than inclination. This inference is based upon the presence of one or more sorcerers in every village.

These shamans, while respected, are feared for the harm it is believed they can bring about. They are not true male witches because the evil they are supposed to cause is insignificant compared with the insatiable hatred of the devil toward mankind. Secondly, the power attributed to the exorcist to bring about illness or torment may be ascribed to natural causes. And finally, if the Indians have or have had dealings with the devil, their language would have a noun for him. They do not have one. Instead, they use the Spanish diablo, pronounced by them diabro because of their inability to enunciate the *l*.

In spite of this, among these natives there are a few individuals who acquire the name and reputation of sorcerers by means of tricks and fanfaronades. They enjoy the title because it is profitable and inspires fear.

In the practice of his witchcraft, a sorcerer will provide himself with grama roots (zacate), pebbles, and charcoal which he carefully conceals. Upon arriving at the bedside of the patient, the sorcerer fans him with large feathers as if driving away flies. Then the sorcerer sucks the aching part, having first dexterously placed in his mouth some of the articles mentioned. After sucking the aching part, the sorcerer produces the objects that were in his mouth and declares, "This is what made you sick." The grama roots look like worms, and he will dispose of all the evidence quickly by throwing it in the fire which is always present in a sickroom regardless of how hot the weather may be.[6]

---

[5] Apparently Nentvig had not heard of, or gave no credence to, the "doll affair" of Agustín Ausculbul in which Father Felipe Ségesser and Capt. Juan Bautista Anza took part during May and June of 1737. Cf. *Memorias de la Academia Mexicana de la historia*. **XXVIII**, 2:150.

[6] Nentvig seems to overlook the writings of his fellow missionary Carlos Roxas, S.J. In his "*Bosquejo histórico . . . de Arizpe,* 28 Julio, 1744." He attributes the death of Marcos de Loyola, S.J., to the supernatural powers of a sorcerer. Loyola died in 1701 casting hairy worms from his nasal passages.

SECTION THREE

Superstitions, Omens, and Credulities

These Indians, as do all simple peoples, at times show signs of superstitions and silly beliefs inherited from their forefathers. I am not convinced that such foolishness is deeply rooted because when enlightened by the missionaries they seem to give them up readily, outwardly at least. Still, who could put an end to their believing that a strong wind foretells the approach of the Apaches? Or that he who dies of a snakebite would have been killed by a thunderbolt had not the snake anticipated the occurrence? Or that the clothing or whatever the bitten one was wearing must be thrown away for if not, the snake will return to bite again? Or that the pouring of an olla full of water over their heads will prevent their being struck by a thunderbolt before the year's end?

These nations, including the Opatas, retained until lately a curious custom known as "plea to the clouds." At nightfall during the rainy season, a number of young girls dressed in white chemises would come out to dance on a well-swept and decorated patch of ground while the older folks would remain in the huts and make mellow sounds with hollowed-out gourds, small sticks, and bones. It was believed that this ritual would make the sky drop its moisture and irrigate their fields. Despite the secrecy of the performance, with God's help this incantation became known to the missionaries. This custom has been discredited and stopped.

During an eclipse they believe it is necessary to make loud noises. They will yell and even ring the church bells if the missionary or any Spaniard is not there to stop them.

In the old days in order to find out the direction from which their enemies would attack, they would catch a certain locust called *hupithui* in their language, and holding it by its head they would ask, "Which way are the enemies coming?" Naturally the little creature so held moved its legs. The questioner took as an answer that the Apaches were approaching in the direction indicated by the first leg which moved. As I understand it, this method is much used by the Apaches themselves.

During thunderstorms when the din of thunder and the flashes of lightning frighten sensible people, these Indians are delighted and leap for joy. I have witnessed this performance several times but have not been able to determine the reason for their jubilation. I believe that their behavior is more of a ceremony than genuine rejoicing.

If a bolt of lightning strikes an Indian, whether he is dead or alive he is never taken home. Instead he is left where he was struck. If he is alive, the relatives supply him with food and drink. If he is dead, the body is left undisturbed for three days while the relatives wait for the frightened soul, supposedly hovering about, to reenter the body. If life does not return, the cadaver is dressed; a hole is dug and the body is buried in a sitting position well supplied with pinole, quelites, etc. The ceremony as described was witnessed by a fellow missionary and shows the drollery and the silliness of the natives.

When it hails, they place an otate cane [solid type of bamboo, *Bamboo arundinacea*], *baquido* in Opata, standing on end at the door of each hut. They firmly believe that the hailing will cease if this is done.

Frequently one finds piles of stones, sticks, bones, etc. beside main roads. It is the custom for those on horseback to throw on these mounds the whips they carry to urge their mounts onward. Those on foot pick up a twig or something from the road and add it to these mounds. Some say that by doing this, the person and his mount as well will be relieved of weariness. Others claim that the piles are burial places of people who have frozen to death, and the piles are burned when it is very cold to warm the souls of the departed. Be that as it may, it is a superstition that ought to be stopped. And since the missionaries cannot stop it, the native magistrates should attempt to do so by imposing penalties for those who add to these piles.

SECTION FOUR

Rites, Customs, and Ceremonies

Drunkenness is not so prevalent among these nations as it is in others. Among the Opatas and Eudebes, the vice has been uprooted by the diligence and vigilance of the missionaries. The Pimas, particularly the upper ones, still indulge. Not having been punished for the uprising of 1751, they have reverted to their heathen ways. The missionaries, to their great sorrow, hampered by the military who have banded together against them instead of opposing the true enemies of God, king, and country, are unable to remedy, or even attempt to remedy the evil.

Their intoxicating beverages made of corn, mezcal, wheat, and Indian figs [tuna] are bad enough, but the elderberry wine is worse because of its lasting effects.

In their gatherings and assemblies they follow their whims unrestrained. An older individual, a warchief, or some presumptuous braggart of a sorcerer, recounts his real or imaginary exploits, often taking all night or until the satanic eulogist becomes hoarse or breathless. I know, because three or four times I have been unable to get out of attending these gatherings, and I have never spent sadder nights. In order that variety may beguile boredom, after the recital there are dances and songs as mournful and doleful as the preceding tale.

After the uprising of 1751 pagan marriages were restored in which the stronger took by force the wives of the weaker whose unions had been sanctified by the Church. These forced unions are called diabro buhuturus, meaning "work of the devil."

Most of their own heathenish betrothals are unfit to be described. However, I will recount the most recent rite as performed in the Pivipa and Jamaica villages of the Tacupeto Valley and at Mortero before its abandonment in 1760.

Old and young gathered together with the prospective grooms assembled in one row and the girls of marriageable age in another, both dressed only in their primitive innocence. At a given signal the young women would start to run and scatter. At a second signal the young men would take up the chase, and upon overtaking the girl of his choice, the young man would seize her left breast. This constituted the nuptial ceremony. Dancing followed, and after a while each couple was placed between two mats made of palm leaves. The singing and dancing continued until daybreak or until the participants reached the point of exhaustion, although in these celebrations the Indians seem tireless.

The newly born, regardless of sex, are submitted to a most painful marring by having the upper and lower eyelids pricked with thorns that contain a black substance which I judge to be finely ground charcoal. A pattern is made which looks like a circle of dots around each eye. The Indians think this enhances beauty. Further disfigurement on the rest of their pitiful bodies is carried out as the children grow older. I have seen an old woman in the Pimería Alta tattooed from neck to waist with what appeared to be numberless strings of beads. The missionaries have tried in vain to eradicate this barbarous custom of our spiritual children.

Another ritual not at all painful to the little ones is that of acquiring foster parents who are called peri. The real parents invite a friend or relative to become the peri, a man for a boy, a woman for a girl. The foster parent then talks to the infant as if the infant were an adult, inciting him or her to be a devoted, vigorous warrior. All the while, the peri runs his hands over the entire body of the child, flexing and stretching the little one's arms and legs. Finally the peri confers his own surname upon the infant by word of mouth. This act is supposed to make them blood relatives. Later on, this relationship must be investigated thoroughly by the missionary before uniting couples in matrimony because this kinship does not make them blood relatives. Occasionally parties distanced by a quarrel use the peri ceremony to get back together.

With the exception of the Apaches, all these nations, both heathen and recently converted, show their devotion to their dead by burying all the deceased's belongings plus some pinole and a jug of water with him. The missionary, attempting to prevent the Pimas, especially the Pimas Altos, from practicing this custom, must remain at the burial site until it is completely closed.

The Apaches are not so painstaking. Regardless of who dies or where death occurs, the body is left to serve as food for wild animals. However, they do attempt to carry away and conceal those who die fighting Christians even if the remains have to be quartered. When a nursing infant dies, for a few successive days a cupful[7] of the mother's milk is thrown in the grave.

---

[7] The word Nentvig uses here is jícara, meaning a dried shell of a gourd, preferably with an elongated neck. Cut in half lengthwise and its contents scooped out, it is used as a ladle. Etymologically it is from the Axtec *xicalli*.

SECTION FIVE

War Practices, Ceremonies, and Rituals

It is customary among the Opatas and presumably among the other nations of Sonora as well that if one is to become a warrior he is required to participate in a few raids against the enemy and accompany some convoys across dangerous territory. After the candidate for warrior has successfully completed these requisites, the warchief assembles the fighting men, armed with bows, arrows, shields, and lances, in the village where the candidate was born. One comes forth out of this gathering to sponsor the aspirant. The sponsor stands behind him while the captain-at-war instructs the intended warrior in the obligations he is about to assume. The aspirant is told he must endure heat, cold, the inclemency of the weather, thirst, and hunger with a stout heart. He is told he must be fearless before the enemy whom he is to look upon with scorn as if they were ants to be trod upon and killed with impudence and courage whenever possible. The lecture over, the captain draws a dried-out eagle's talon from his quiver. With it he begins clawing a zig-zag course down the youth's arm from shoulder to wrist, cutting deeply enough to draw blood. Then this same procedure is followed on the other arm, the chest and legs. The aspirant must endure this without a whimper. However, a tear rolling down his cheek will not prevent his being accepted as a warrior. Upon completion of the cutting of his body, he receives a bow, quiver, and arrows, symbols of his newly attained rank. Immediately following this, the sponsor and each of the fighting men contribute two additional arrows.

When actually in the field, the newly accepted member is put through additional tests of fortitude which are selected for him. He is given the least desirable and most onerous tasks, such as guarding the horses at night, and regardless of the weather he must remain without shelter and away from the warming fire. Should this newest warrior resent his treatment, his fellow warriors abuse him more by dousing him from head to foot with cold water. All his troubles are ended when a new candidate joins the company. The new warrior needs rugged training, for when he is in pursuit of the Apaches he must be heedless of storms and rain and freezing weather. Fires must not be lit in this situation.

The warriors always attack at dawn, approaching silently and catching the enemy by surprise. The enemy will flee, leaving behind weapons and any plunder they may have. The attackers instead of pursuing the enemy waste time scalping the dead and celebrating their triumph.

When called to campaign against the enemy, the Opatas and the Eudebes take eight days to prepare, although they could be ready much sooner. On the eve of their departure they will ask the missionary for a mount, or a blanket, or something that they suddenly feel they might need. Once these final wishes have been fulfilled, instead of going home to rest, they go to the community center where the warchief chatters at them until dawn, the starting time. The expedition is usually composed of a few Spanish soldiers and Indians from several villages. As they travel, they stop at various pueblos and repeat these nightly performances. The warriors claim, and convincingly so, that they prepare themselves to be alert if a nocturnal attack should occur. However, recurrent sleepless nights do not make them more alert.

Upon their return the victorious Indians celebrate day and night with the enemy scalps they have brought back. And they force their captives, women and children, to witness their antics. It is pitiful to see them waste their energy and undermine their health with such madness. And it is even worse to see the abuse they heap upon their captives who are compelled to endure fatigue and sleeplessness during the endless performance. While in Sáric before the 1751 revolt I saw a beautiful Apache child die of exhaustion. She was captured in a Gila River foray, and just before the end I had the consolation of baptizing her.

In some Opata pueblos this tribe, which is believed to be the most submissive, practices a brutal custom: old women carrying burning sticks scorch parts of the captives' bodies, chiefly the thighs. I have seen the scars of this inhumane cruelty upon a boy of tender age. Doubtless these ruthless acts were known to the Spanish officers.[8]

---

[8] Nentvig implies that the Spanish officers tolerated this brutality.

Upon returning to their village, the warriors are received in accordance with the success they have attained. If nothing has been achieved, they return at night quietly. But if all has gone well and they have a few scalps and other spoils, an advance messenger goes to the pueblo with the news, and a reception is planned for the daylight hours. The warriors are met by the women folk headed by the mate of the chieftain or some other elderly one. After an exchange of greetings and congratulations for having punished the enemy upon his very soil, a scalp is snatched by the female leader who displays it as a trophy and begins chanting. The other women join in this chant which is a ballad composed for such an event. The ballad exaggerates insultingly the enemy's defeat and decries their improvidence and laziness that made them resort to raiding and killing. Meanwhile the scalp is being passed from one individual to another and is subjected to indecorous actions: ashes and hot water are thrown upon it; it is stamped upon, while the warriors merely witness the macabre rites, remaining inactive spectators.

When the warriors return to their homes, they will hang their weapons by the door before entering. As for the booty, be it clothing, household belongings, or food, it is divided among the women and the older men who were unable to join in the fighting. The warriors do not share in the spoils. They believe that if they make use of any part of it, they will soon be killed by the Apaches. However, they are beginning to set this qualm aside, and at present they will even make use of the weapons they have captured.

Among some of the wilder Opatas and Eudebes it was customary to chop off a hand of a dead enemy, bring it to the village and treat it much like the scalp. Furthermore, it was used to stir the pinole drink which was partaken by those present, including Spaniards if invited. This custom, a vengeful demonstration against their Apache enemy, is rapidly disappearing at the behest of the missionaries who continually represent it and the rite of scalping as an atheistic, filthy, and loathsome practice inherited from their barbaric ancestors.

But enough of this folly. Let us deal with their treatment of wounds.

SECTION SIX

Treatment of Wounds

As a supplement to what has been said about the Indians' treatment of illnesses, let us deal with the treatment of arrow wounds. The lesion is first sucked, then powdered peyote [*Lophophora williamsii*], *pejori* in Opata, is applied deep into the wound. Every two days the wound is cleansed with a cotton-tipped stick, and more peyote powder is applied. Later lechuguilla powder, *cu* in Opata, is used. Nothing more is done, and the wound heals.

For wounds not of the thorax or belly, healing is accomplished by the daily application of a salve obtained either from the century plant [mezcal or maguey], lechuguilla[9] [an agave], date palm, or the echo [pipe stem cactus]. This salve is prepared in the same manner as the romerillo[10] and is introduced into the wound as deeply as possible by means of wicks.

And as thirst torments the wounded no less than the pain of the injury, this province offers splendid refreshments: one may strip off the sharp thorns and rough cortical layer of the echo, or tesejo as it is sometimes called, and chew the pulp of the tenderest shoots. These shoots yield sufficient juice to appease thirst as well as hunger that may assail the individual who is isolated. The taste may not be to his liking, but as the adage says, "To the famished, the quality of food is unimportant."[11] Another efficacious remedy to allay thirst which is provided by the creator of all Nature is the root of pochote[12] [*Ceiba pentandra*], *sabó* in Opata. When chewed, this stimulates the flow of saliva, and the chewer soon finds his mouth watering. And still another cactus that offers relief from thirst when chewed is cholla, *tepo* in Opata [*Opuntia thurberi*].

---

[9] There are many plants of the agave family with this name.

[10] This is described in chapter iv, section two.

[11] "Para buena hambre nada es mala comida."

[12] This is not the *pochote* described by Pfefferkorn. It is probably *xiloxochitl, Bombax ellipticum,* described by Hernández in *Historia de las plantas* . . . **II,** *p. 453.*

VI

Tribes of Sonora

SECTION ONE
Opatas, Eudebes, and Jovas

Because they are village dwellers, the Opatas and some of the Eudebes are regarded as more advanced than those who remain in isolated huts. These village dwellers, while retaining their status as Indians, are more amenable to reason. They are the best Christians and the most loyal vassals of the king, having never rebelled against him or the missionaries. They are the truest and bravest in war, aiding the royal troops when they are campaigning against the common enemy. Moreover, they are more inclined to till the soil and breed livestock.

They obtain good crops of wheat, maize, beans, pumpkins, melons, etc., but because they do not value their labor, they sell their produce for a trifle. They are so fond of trading that when their customers[1] ask for something they do not have, they will beg it from the missionary using one excuse or another in order to complete the trade and usually they end up with less.

While the Opata women join the men in everyday labors, when pregnant they are treated with more consideration than in other provinces. They cease doing heavy work and devote themselves to cooking pozole,[2] roasting or popping corn,[3] grinding it to make pinole, spinning cotton, and weaving.

---

[1] The word Nentvig uses here is *noraguas* (singular form is *noragua*) which is loosely applied by the Opatas to mean friend, friendship, or business client.

[2] A stew made of hominy, wheat, peas, beans, and fresh or salted meat.

[3] Esquite.

Thus, to the Opata women has come the gift that the Vulgate calls "the instinct of the cock,"[4] and the Septuagint[5] interprets *"Quis dedit mulieribus texturae sapientiam aut variegativam scientiam?"*[6] They are happy in the knowledge that while their sisters with the Pimas Altos and Apaches are compelled to slave in the fields, they perform more feminine duties. Although their equipment is rudimentary, the Opata women weave so expertly that no one can surpass them. If permitted to unravel a sample, they could imitate German tablecloths and napkins, the only difference being the coarseness of the Indian material. The high quality of craftsmanship is the reason their finished pieces are called alemaniscos.[7] They can imitate any texture, even tent cloth.

Their weaving is done in the following manner: First they drive four stakes into the ground far enough apart to accommodate the length and width of the work planned. Next they tie a slender twig horizontally half a yard above the ground to each of the sides thus limiting the width. Then with a woman on each of the width sides facing each other, they begin the warping, passing a skein of thread around the horizontal twigs as many times as necessary to block out the work. This done, and with the sample before them, they begin counting the threads, catching two at a time by means of a wooden rod. They mark the divisions of the texture and make them secure by means of wooden slats. Then a stick serves as a woof and carries the transverse strand which is tightened by small wooden picks. Thus by constant repetition the work proceeds slowly and tediously regardless of entreaties to use a loom to simplify and expedite their ways. It is useless to struggle to make the natives change their methods. Their patience can tire the world. They refuse to try anything that is different, and this unwillingness applies to other tasks as well, such as turning and clearing the soil, etc.

---

[4] Job 38:36.

[5] A pre-Christian Greek version of the Old Testament named for the approximate number of its translators.

[6] "Who has given to women the knowledge of weaving and such a many-sided wisdom?"

[7] German imitations.

In this respect the newly converted Pimas are more cooperative than the Opatas. The Opatas are quite sure they have nothing more to learn, and they continue their crude, primitive ways. But the Pimas recognize their limitations and obediently submit to our teachings. The backward state of affairs prevails among those not in contact with the missionaries, and when I asked an old man why the corn fields of the nonconverted had not been weeded, he replied, "They still have their eyes closed." Generally speaking this is true of all the Sonoran Indians. Quite naturally there are exceptions. Along certain lines the Indian's application and natural ability make him proficient, for example in playing musical instruments, carpentering, blacksmithing, stone-cutting, and even house-building.

I know of a few Opatas and Eudebes who are proficient in as many as nine crafts. They do not learn by taking lessons and practicing the rules of the art, but rather they learn by taking a liking to a trade and seeing it done once or twice. Then they go forth and do it themselves. We often say that they are capable of learning by seeing plus the application of their natural ability to use their hands. The Opatas built the flour mills of Don Juan Terán at Pivipa as well as the mills of Father José Cabrera Roldán, S.J., at Arivechi and Father Javier Villaroya at Banámichi. What has been said of the Opatas is applicable to the Eudebes except that the latter have to try harder to abandon their old ways.

The Jovas as a tribe are wilder, more ignorant, and less disposed to live in townsites, preferring the mountain ravines where they were born to the good treatment and comforts they could enjoy in the pueblos. This was proven by Father Manuel Aguirre, S.J., of Bacadéhuachi when he attempted to move them from their rancherías at Sátechi, Pónida, Teópari, and Mochopa where they are sustaining themselves with roots, herbs, wild fruits, and an occasional harvest of corn, and occupying themselves by making mats from the fronds of the many palm trees that grow in that area. These they sell or exchange for the little clothing they wear. And the women manage to weave wool from the few sheep they raise to make blankets, capes, jackets, and breaches for the men and shawls, skirts, chemises, and waistcoats for themselves.

They pose no threat to their fellow tribesmen who have submitted to the more normal life. At the same time they are fearless against the Apaches, and in 1760 one of them named Salvador defended his wife and three children against seven enemies from daybreak to sundown. He killed four Apaches. Finally, sapped by hunger and exhaustion, he surrendered and perished at the hands of the surviving three savages.

The substance used by the Jovas to poison arrows is so deadly that it kills the wounded as well as those who attempt to suck the poison from the lesion. Years ago in an encounter of nine Apaches against three Jovas, three Apaches were wounded and the remaining six, wishing to help, sucked the wounds, and all died. An Opata woman who was their prisoner escaped and told what had happened.

The Opatas, Pimas, and Jovas inhabit the greater part of Sonora. They are found on the south at Nátora, Arivechi, Bacanora, Tónichi, Soyopa, Nácori, and [Los] Alamos; on the west they live at Ures, Nacameri, Opodepe, and Cucurpe; on the north from Cucurpe through Arizpe, Chinapa, Bacoachi, Cuquiárachi to Bavispe, and on the east from Bavispe through the western slopes of the Sierra Madre Occidental down to Nátora. May it please God that some way be found to bring the Indians down from their craggy, mountain strongholds to the plains where there are tillable lands and where their souls can better be instructed in our Holy Faith.

SECTION TWO

Pimas Altos and Bajos

The Pima nation[8] is a large one. An entire description will not be undertaken because some of its pueblos are in other provinces. For example, Yécora is in Chínipas; Guasave is in Sinaloa, and still other pueblos are in Tarahumara. I have knowledge of the Pima pueblos in Tarahumara because I have read about them in the work of Father Pérez Ribas, whose book I do not possess.

We shall begin with the Pimas Bajos by naming the missions and their locations which serve as landmarks in the territory. On the south

[8] It is divided by geographical location into upper and lower.

are Taraichi, Cumuripa, Onapa, Nuri, Movas, and Onavas; on the west, actually serving as barriers to Seri incursions, are Cumuripa, Suaqui,[9] San José, Santa Rosalía, Ures, and Nacameri.[10]

Having heard that others had become Christians,[11] the Pimas Bajos traveled south to receive instruction in the Faith, thus becoming the first Sonorans to be converted. However, the Pimas Bajos lack meekness. And their loyalty is very weak. There is much evil to be uprooted here.

The territory occupied by the Pimas Altos may be defined by the following boundaries: on the south Cucurpe, Santa Ana, and Caborca to the Gulf of California; on the east from Cucurpe to Dolores, Remedios, Cocóspera, and the Terrenate presidio. From there it follows the San Pedro River—also known as the Sobahipuris—to its junction with the Gila. On the north it follows the course of the Gila, including both banks, to the Colorado; and the western boundary is formed by the Gulf of California. Thus their territory measures from east to west sixty to 130 leagues and from northwest to southeast more or less 130 leagues. It is true that all of the expanse from Caborca to the mouth of the Colorado is uninhabited or uninhabitable because it is extremely sandy, and the plains are very windy. Moreover, the region is arid, and the soil is barren. In fact, in the last thirty leagues before one reaches the Colorado there is a total absence of water. In this area about fifty leagues to the northwest of Caborca is the mission of San Miguel de Sonoitac. Established in May, 1751,[12] it is attended by a few Papagos,[13] who sustain themselves by eating grass seed, herbs, wild fruits, rabbits, and mice. One cannot really call this group at San Miguel de Sonoitac a congregation. Not until one reaches Tucson,

---

[9] This is Zuaqui on Nentvig's map.

[10] Eastern and northern boundaries are not given in the text.

[11] These were Zuaquis of the province of Sinaloa.

[12] Most likely Nentvig meant that the mission of San Miguel de Sonoitac was reestablished in 1751. Father Kino had visited the area in October of 1698, and some sort of church was erected there in 1701. Father Sedelmayr installed Father Enrique Ruhen there in May, 1751. Father Ruhen was killed on November 20 or 21 of that same year.

[13] A subdivision of the Upper Pimas, also called Papapootans.

Santa Catalina, Baigatz,[14] etc., to the Gila, does one see the possibility of extending the faith and the dominions of our king.

The Pimas Altos may be subdivided into four groups:

1. those living in villages;[15]
2. the above mentioned Papagos;
3. the Sobahipuris, with Soba as their chief;
4. the Gileños, who as the name implies reside on both banks of the Gila River. Included in this group may be the Opas, Cocomaricopas, Hud-Coadans, Yumas, Cuhuanas, and Quiquimas, who inhabit the lands beyond the Colorado-Gila junction.

All of these groups speak the same dialect with only slight variations. [In this, Nentvig errs. Cf. footnote 22, chapter II.]

Because the Pimas Altos are the newest converts to the faith, and because those who have been converted still have dealings with the unconverted of their tribe, the converts are unstable, more barbarous, and firmly attached to their heathen customs, superstitions, debaucheries, and indecent dances. They are the least loyal and cruelest, for no others have killed so many innocents and missionaries. During their insurrections they have brought cruel deaths to three members of the Society of Jesus who were outstanding and fervent workers in the vineyard of the Lord.[16]

In courage all the Pimas are inferior to the Opatas, and only when they have large numbers do they show boldness and daring. This was demonstrated in the uprising of 1751 when a large group of them were frenzied with a thirst for blood. They reduced the finely decorated church of Sáric to ashes, then went on to Tubutama where only ten men, half of whom had no knowledge of firearms, held them in check. For two days they attacked the house in which fathers Sedelmayr and Nentvig had taken refuge. After the attacking band had lost a few men, they were frightened and for a time did not resume the

[14] These villages are along the Santa Cruz River, and were so named by Father Kino on January 13, 1687.

[15] Their villages border the San Miguel and Sonora rivers.

[16] Nentvig is referring to Father Saéta in 1695 and fathers Tello and Ruhen in 1751.

fight. This gave time for the besieged to escape, leaving behind three who were so badly wounded they could not travel. These three were put to death by the rebels.

Also, a group of ten soldiers, one of whom was Don Gabriel Vildósola, captain of the Fronteras presidio, advanced to Aribaca to recover camp goods, totally unaware of the insurrection. They suddenly found themselves facing 200 daring rebels. The troops were able to retreat in good order without suffering any casualties.

The Pimas, numbering 5,000 to 6,000 armed men, gathered at Babuquíburi, a hill beyond Aribaca. Captain Don Bernardo Urrea, then lieutenant governor of the Upper Pima region, arrived and could have subdued them in two hours, but he was constrained by orders from the governor of the province, Don Diego Ortiz Parrilla, to bring about their surrender by peaceful means. Paying no heed to the inducements to lay down their arms, the rebellious Pimas attacked furiously, and in spite of their vastly superior numbers they could not "have for breakfast" the royal force as promised by their captain-general Luis.[17] Defeated, they were forced to flee farther inland.

In addition to the bow and arrow, the Pimas have the *macana,* a heavy, hardwood club used in hand-to-hand combat. It is capable of breaking a head with one blow. This is the instrument used to kill Father Tomás Tello of Caborca.

Among the Pimas, the most inured to war are the Sobahipuris who have been reared on the Apache frontier and are used to almost constant fighting. However, in 1762, being tired of frequent battles, they abandoned their pleasant and fertile valley. Some migrated south to Santa María Soamca while others went farther southwest to Guebavi and Sonoitac,[18] and still others traveled west to San Xavier del Bac and Tucson, thus leaving free ingress to the whole Upper Pimería to the Apache enemy.

Were it not for fear of the Apaches, two or three missions might have been established in the Sobahipuris Valley which in time would

---

[17] This is Luis Oacpicasigua, more commonly referred to as Luis de Sáric.

[18] Not San Miguel de Sonoitac but San Ignacio de Sonoitac, also known as San Ignacio de los Sobahipuris or Los Reyes de Sonoitac. On Nentvig's map this is located at 33 degrees north latitude, 263 degrees, 30 minutes west longitude.

have brought about communication with the rancherías on the north bank of the Gila River.

We have already hinted that if we wished to populate the western side of the San Pedro River, we would have to do so with the little-to-be-trusted Papagos who cannot easily be induced to settle in villages. During the last uprising they were supporters of the petty chief Luis de Sáric who, on November 20, 1751, was encamped in a ravine half a league from Sáric. This I learned from an eyewitness who spoke the truth. If I had not believed him and had passed through that ravine, it would have cost me my life.

Let us put an end to the subject of the Pimas because if I were to write all that suggests itself, it would require the steeping of the pen in blood, which I wish to avoid so far as it is consistent with the truth and the simplicity of my nature.

SECTION THREE

The Seris and Their Confederates

With the exception of the Guaymas of whom enough has already been said,[19] the Seris are the smallest tribe in the province. Their small numbers were demonstrated when they were gathered together and only one mission could be established, which was named Nuestra Señora del Pópulo. Father Nicolás Perera, S.J., the missionary who for the longest time bore their insolence, told me that he never saw more than 300 gathered together at one time. And I do not even know where he could have seen that many.

They are the most cruel and uninhibited, always wild and rebellious to the law of God, even those who had been confined to the pueblos of Pópulo, Nacameri, and Los Angeles—actually only a small part of the tribe. But even these few managed to have daily communications with their heathen relatives. As if no one were suspicious, the converted ones would travel to other communities and learn what they wanted to know. Then the information would be passed on to the unconverted who carried out crimes with such precision, timeliness, and accuracy that people were astonished. Many times suspicion

[19] Chapter v, section one.

would fall on the Pópulo Seris who would rapidly clear themselves by proving with eyewitnesses that at the very hour the outrage occurred they were in such and such a place. So to curb the Seri movements, the presidios of Pitic and Terrenate were founded at the end of 1741 or the beginning of 1742 by order of his excellency the Viceroy, Count of Fuenclara, acting with the concurrence of the Ministers of War and the Exchequer.

In 1748 during the administration of Don José Rafael Rodríguez Gallardo, executive-visitor of Sonora,[20] the Pitic presidio was moved to San Miguel, a site located one and a half leagues southwest of El Pópulo but still on the communal lands farmed by the people of that village. It cannot be denied that the moving of the presidio and the dividing up of the Pópulo communal land amongst the residents of the fort angered the Seris. Their dissatisfaction was manifested by the havoc they created shortly afterward. Up to that time the Seris had not been so unruly. With the assurance that their land would be returned, some eighty families settled in Pópulo, and there were hopes that the rest of the tribe would follow.

But these hopes were lost in 1750 when the Seri residents of Pópulo were unexpectedly arrested and their women deported. The men were sent away in chains but were able to escape, and one by one they returned to take vengeance for the indignities they suffered. As we shall see, their hostility resulted in a sharp reduction of the population.[21]

However, by the end of 1753 the Seris began to listen to peace overtures made by the recently arrived governor Don Pablo Arce y Arroyo. Their peace envoys demanded the return of the scattered Seri women who had been sent away to Guatemala and other parts of the continent, the return of their lands at Pópulo and Los Angeles, the

---

[20] This title in Spanish is juez-pesquisidor. This is sometimes translated as visitor-general but means literally investigating judge. The magistrate was appointed to inquire and correct. That is, he not only had the authority to make recommendations, he had the power to act.

[21] The arrest referred to was ordered by Governor Diego Ortiz Parrilla, whose campaign against the Seris took place between September 14 and October 2, 1750. Father Francisco Antonio Pimentel, chaplain of the expedition, wrote a complete report in *Boletín del Archivo General de la Nación* **XVII,** 4 (1946):503–74.

moving of the presidio back to Pitic, and the assigning of Father Nicolás Perera as their missionary.

Because the governor had to be elsewhere on an inspection tour, he sent fathers Felipe Ségesser and Nicolás Perera as his representatives. They offered the Seris hope and promised to do everything possible to comply with three of their demands, but locating and returning the Seri women seemed an impossible task. The envoys could offer little here. And the Seris wanted a clear-cut promise.

Father Perera invited Chepillo, their chief, to a private conference, and when the brave Seri chieftain came to Aconchi at night, they had a heart-to-heart talk. When Father Perera asked him to submit to the demands of the governor, Chepillo said, "I know that if we continue fighting we are damning ourselves, but there is no other way. We are accustomed to living with women. We do not know where our wives are, whether they are living or dead. You would not marry us to others, and if we take others, you will order us whipped. It is not our fault but that man's."[22] So saying, he took his leave. In January, 1754, I heard Father Perera relate the episode, and during the recounting he could not restrain his tears.

During the time the peace negotiations were gong on, the Guaymas attacked a Seri ranch-hamlet, killing some of the residents and mistreating others. Even though no Spaniards had taken part in the raid, the Seris said, "If this happens when the peace talks are going on, what assurance do we have that incidents will not occur after the talks are concluded?" They were told that it was neither the fault of the governor nor any Spaniard. The Guaymas, living in a distant part of the country, had not been aware of the negotiations, and what had happened had been an unforeseen accident. The most that could be obtained from the Seris was that hostilities would cease while their demands were being met. And during Governor Arce's tenure the promise was kept. But no sooner had the late governor Don Juan Antonio Mendoza taken the reins of the government than bloodshed and fire began to devastate the province.[23]

---

[22] The reference is to the former governor, Parrilla.

[23] Nentvig refers to the "late governor Mendoza" because this magistrate had been killed on November 27, 1760, by the Seri Chief Becerro at a place in the vicinity of Saracachi.

During Governor Arce's term of office Seri rustling of cattle and horses continued but in a different way: the Indians left their tired mounts behind and respected the lives of the ranchers. By comparison with past deeds, this practice could be called gentlemanly and courteous.

Even though they have suffered the loss of some forty vagrants and over seventy women and children who were captured in the encounters of November and December of this past year, 1761, they remain arrogant and unwilling to accept the pacts offered to them. May it please the Lord that the royal forces sent to subdue them will succeed in obtaining the peace and tranquility so necessary to prevent the complete ruin of Sonora. Once this is accomplished, our scant forces could be used to oppose the other and greater enemy, the Apaches.

The principal refuge of the Seris is the famous Cerro Prieto, twelve leagues west of San José de Pimas, an equal distance south of Pitic, fourteen leagues from the Gulf of California, and thirty leagues north of the Yaqui River. This retreat is an aggregate of many pinnacles, an almost impregnable fortress with innumerable chasms, canyons, and deep precipices inaccessible to the cavalry. Even when the enemy has been routed and the Seris are in full retreat, the cavalry cannot penetrate this stronghold. The twists and turns of the narrow trails permit the Seris to reach unassailable positions among the towering mountain peaks.

The lesser canyons will not be mentioned here. The best known are the Cosari, facing east; the Rodríguez to the northeast; the Grande, facing northeast; the Palma directly north; the Cara Pintada to the northwest; the Otates to the west-northwest; the Nopalera to the west; Las Avispas to the west-southwest; La Ciénega to the southwest; and finally the Rincón de Marcos, facing southeast. The range which contains the Cerro Prieto extends south toward the small village of San José de Guaymas. [These canyons are clearly marked on Nentvig's map.]

In addition to the Cerro Prieto which has been a Seri sanctuary for the last four or five years, the mountain of Bacoachi Grande sixteen leagues west of San Miguel de Horcasitas, the Cerro de las Espuelas some leagues beyond, and Picú, a range of mountains along the coast, were occasionally used as Seri shelters. But these were less intricate and the royal troops had easier access to them. The Seris were driven from these places with some loss of life and no longer feel safe in these haunts.

Other Seri shelters were the Tiburón Island, nearly forty leagues west of Pitic and one league from the coast, and San Juan Bautista Island,[24] nine leagues southeast of the former and two leagues from the coast. To the north of Tiburón lies the Ensenada de Tepoca that in years past was renowned for its pearl beds and was called Placer de Tepoca. On the Sonora coast north of the bays of Guaymas and San Javier there is no known harbor other than the harbor of Santa Clara at almost 33 degrees north latitude. And even this is doubtful because of the vagueness of Father Kino's writings.[25]

The substance used by the Seris to poison their arrows is the most active known hereabout. If treatment as described above is not begun at once, even if the wound is superficial the area around it swells and the poison soon spreads throughout the body. The skin breaks; the flesh falls away, and the victim dies within 24 hours.

According to information given to me by an old man who in more peaceful times used to dive for pearls at the Placer de Tepoca where he had seen the poison prepared, the process is the same as that employed by the Caberres Indians of the Orinoco as described by Padre José Gumilla in his book, Volume II, Chapter 12, except that the Seris test their poison more cautiously. First, the arm or thigh of a lad is cut with a flint, and the blood is allowed to flow for some distance. The blood is touched with a poisoned tip, and if the blood seethes and draws back, the poison is just right. The streak of blood is then wiped with the hand so that death may not be introduced through the veins of the subject.

---

[24] This is now called San Estéban Island. Over a mile long and not quite two square miles in total area with mountain peaks reaching 1600 feet, it is located three miles southwest of the larger Tiburón Island in the Gulf of California. Currently it is uninhabited.

[25] This has been identified by Bolton as Adair Bay. In 1937 a topographer, Jorge López Collada, and three assistants lost their lives while surveying the course of the railroad, then under construction, that runs from Sonora to Baja California. In his memory the Santa Clara inlet, also known as Adair Bay, was renamed López Collada Bay (Bahía López Collada).

A second difference between the two poisons is that nothing is known of the composition of the Seri poison. Some say that it is made from the heads of irritated vipers cut off at the very moment they sink their fangs into a piece of lung or semi-decomposed human flesh or other filthiness. All of this is merely conjecture, and I refuse to provoke the wrath of the reader with more of it. Doubtless some venomous herb serves as the main ingredient.

And thank God, the third and last difference is that the Seri venom does not take effect instantly. There is time for the application of remedies, and there are several besides that of the caramatraca mentioned in chapter iv, section three. At least if the treatment is not successful, the patient has time to prepare for death in a Christian manner.

We ought to thank the Divine Providence on another score: the Seris have not divulged the secret of their poison to their allies the Pimas.[26] Whether the Seris have discontinued using poisoned arrows because the Pimas have or whether the Seris have discontinued their use because the Indian auxiliaries of the royal forces often shoot them back is not known, but the fact remains that for the last two or three years ravages from poisoned arrows have not been experienced.

Having referred to the Pimas as the allies of the Seris, one must explain that besides the loyal Pimas Altos who were staunch followers of the Faith, there were the unconverted members of the same tribe who continued on the warpath even after the uprising of 1751, perpetrating murder and devastation in spite of the continual diligence of our troops and their auxiliaries, who were the faithful ones of the Pimas Altos.

Until 1762 the Seris had nearly always emerged victorious over the government forces. Nevertheless they realized they were losing ground. There was a shortage of women, and a few warriors perished in each encounter, so the need for allies was acute. Therefore, they gladly accepted the unconverted members of the Pimas Altos, who had up to that time been their bitter and irreconcilable enemy. Necessity supplied the bond that affection would not.

---

[26] The Pimas had employed poisoned arrows, and their use in 1696 was recorded by Kino in *Las Misiones,* p. 62, as well as Mange in *Luz de tierra incógnita,* p. 259.

The outcast Pimas Altos, having no safe place in their own territory, endured horrible suffering during the campaign waged against them this past year, 1761. The military maneuvers had been decided upon at a council of war in which Governor Don José Tienda de Cuervo and four captains of the province participated, each subscribing one thousand pesos for their execution.[27] To this campaign the Jesuit missions contributed 560 fanegas of pinole worth four pesos each, and 220 quintales[28] of jerked beef at six pesos each, which made the donation equal to 3,560 pesos.

When the royal troops discovered their lair in the Cosari Canyon, the Pimas were not pursued as relentlessly as they might have been because false hopes were raised in a parley with the commander of our troops. At this meeting, held on an inaccessible mountain peak, the outcasts lied with every word they uttered, ingeniously misrepresenting the cause of the 1751 insurrection. The soldiers and their auxiliaries present were aware of the falseness of their assertions. I as well as many others still living could have refuted every one of their statements. I was astounded that the commander could believe them. The brutal Indians had been caught with the bodies of their murdered victims.[29]

The loyal Pima auxiliaries were disgusted with the result of the parley. Nonetheless the treacherous Pimas were permitted to retain a force of seventy warriors. Soon after, I heard that their numbers were greatly increased by new arrivals from the Upper Pimería, probably Papagos. However, unless the land is cleared entirely of the united bands of Seris and Pimas, regardless of how few they might be, peace will not be achieved. Bad Indians are never lacking in the settlements, and these, fearful of the punishment they deserve, will go over to the rebellious side. Thus, there will always be training grounds for robbers and murderers.

---

[27] Col. Tienda de Cuervo was appointed governor on January 16, 1761, and had disbanded the Pima-Seri hordes by August of that year. The unnamed captains may have been Bernardo Urrea, Gabriel Antonio Vildósola, Juan Bautista Anza, and Francisco Elías González.

[28] Quintal is a unit of weight equal to 100 pounds.

[29] Most likely Nentvig is referring to the assassinations of fathers Enrique Ruhen and Tomás Tello and the destruction of their mission churches.

SECTION FOUR

The Apaches, Ancient Scourge of Sonora

Although the region that is considered to be the land of the Apaches lies beyond the boundaries of Sonora, I deem it advisable to include all the available information so that the reader may become aware of their number, power, and the inconceivable damage this cruel enemy brings about, almost causing the ruin of this province.

According to Father Sedelmayr, their main lair was beyond the Sierra de los Apaches, farther north than latitude 35 degrees, 40 minutes,[30] and their incursions extended east to west from the new presidio [El Paso] del Norte through the presidios of Janos, Fronteras, and Terrenate to the junction of the Asunción and Gila rivers, a distance of over 100 leagues, and from north to south not fewer than 150 leagues.[31]

And those who infest New Mexico are of this same nation, as may be determined by the brands which are on the animals they herd from Sonora to be sold there. In fact their field of action is much greater and extends over a larger area than many of the European kingdoms. Their mode of life, however, is entirely different. They are savagely cruel, and when left to themselves they will kill one another. This has been ascertained by our own soldiers. Nomadic in character, they are in one place today and in another tomorrow. A young boy of five or six told me how his father had been killed and he, the boy, had been left tied to a tree when the Indians moved on to another place. They depend upon the products of the land which are available at each place: tunas, dates, agaves, etc. However, their women remain in a section of the Florida Valley to plant maize, tan horse and deer hides, make jackets, breeches, and sandals of chamois leather, etc. When in camp, the men do nothing but hunt and amuse themselves while the women do this work for them.

All Apache clothing is made of chamois leather. Men wear either a jacket to the waist or a pair or two of skins hung from the shoulders as

---

[30] This is located at 261 degrees, 31 minutes longitude on Nentvig's map.

[31] The presidios referred to were as follows: El Paso del Norte (Ciudad Juárez since 1889) was established in 1685, and there was nothing new about it in 1762. San Felipe y Santiago de Janos was founded in 1686. Fronteras (Santa Rosa de Corodéhuachi) was founded in 1692. Terrenate was founded in 1741.

a sort of double-breasted cape, short breeches and sandals which are made to measure. Women are limited to wearing short mantles which fasten at the neck, scarcely covering their breasts, and skirts which cover from the waist to the knees. Because both men and women go sandaled from infancy, their feet are smaller than those of other Indians, thus leaving easily recognizable tracks.

The women are skilled at riding horses. They are able to leap upon a colt with no bridle other than a thin rope halter. With only this they are able to control and restrain their mounts.

From information gathered from former captives, I have learned that the tribe does not worship idols.

Even though they are scattered over a large area, one surmises their vast numbers by the many raids which occur simultaneously in this province. At the same time they are plundering in Sonora there are war parties of two to three hundred in the Pimería Alta. And there are about the same number raising havoc in Janos, and still others bringing ruin and desolation as far as the interior of Nueva Vizcaya while others are active in Chihuahua. At the same time there are still Apaches in their many rancherías guarding their women and children. Therefore, it is not beyond the realm of probability that their numbers exceed one thousand families.

It is God's merciful design that the Apaches scatter their forces over a large area and do not as a unit attack us, for there could be no place within the entire province that could be held against a united Apache effort. The whole province could be destroyed within a year. This is something to fear because the enemy is changing his tactics. Previously they attacked only two or three times a year always at full moon. Now they attack at any time and in larger numbers. They come in the dark when they are least expected, and the ranchers are negligent in keeping watch. Moreover, the marauders have no fear of our troops and in their retreat are able to reach a mountain stronghold where they have time to rest a stolen herd.

Because this enemy goes unpunished, he is able to keep this normally wealthy province impoverished. The spirit of its dwellers is undermined by the ever present threat of death. Mining and commerce are at a low ebb, and the royal treasury is profitless, all because of the hostile Apaches.

VII

The Jesuit Missions

The missions in the province of Sonora extend from the Yaqui River to the interior of the Pimería Alta and are administered by the Society of Jesus. These missions are under the jurisdiction of a father visitor or superior, so-called because he must visit each church in his territory one or more times during his term of office in much the same way the provincial must visit the colleges within the country assigned to him. At present there are thirty-three missions in Sonora grouped into four rectorships. They are San Francisco de Borja with eight dependent missions, the Santos Mártires del Japón with six, the San Francisco Javier with seven, and the Nuestra Señora de los Dolores in the Upper Pima country with ten.[1] The head of each group is called rector, and he exerts the same authority over the missionaries in his rectorship in this far-flung and semideserted land as the dean of any college does over the students.

SECTION ONE
San Francisco de Borja Rectorship

For the most part this rectorship covers the province of Ostimuri and is just west of the province of Chínipas[2] at almost 29 degrees latitude and 278 degrees longitude.

Its main mission is Onapa. It is administered by Father Jesuit Miguel de Almela and has Taraichi as a dependent mission thirteen

[1] These total thirty-one, not thirty-three as Nentvig states.

[2] At present Chínipas is in the state of Chihuahua.

leagues to the east. Onapa is fifteen leagues northwest of Yécora which is in the province of Chínipas. Twelve leagues south of Onapa is the real SS Trinidad [SS stands for Santísima, meaning most holy], and four leagues north is the real of Tacupeto.

The next principal mission is Arivechi which is seven leagues north-northwest of Onapa at 29 degrees, 17 minutes latitude and 266 degrees, 54 minutes longitude. It is administered by Father Jesuit José Roldán[3] and has two dependent missions. The first is Pónida which is not more than a league to the north-northeast. It is inhabited by Jovas who moved from the now deserted village of Nátora in the east. The second dependent mission is Bacanora which lies nine leagues to the west. Arivechi is inhabited by Eudebe Indians, who are also called Heguis, and by quite a number of Spaniards and gente de razón.

Sahuaripa is the next main mission, lying four leagues north of Arivechi at 29 degrees, 4 minutes latitude and 266 degrees, 54 minutes longitude. It is administered by Father Tomás Pérez [de la Busta] and has Teópari as a dependent mission. Sahuaripa also embraces the ranches of [San Cayetano de] Chamada [Chamata on Nentvig's map] seven leagues beyond Teópari and [San Juan de Dios de] Chipafora eight leagues north-northeast of Sahuaripa itself as well as the village of Santo Tomás just south to which the inhabitants of Chamada had been moved. Its parishioners belong to the Jova nation.

The main mission of Movas lies almost 28 degrees latitude and 266 degrees, 5 minutes longitude; it is administered by the Jesuit Bernardo Middendorff. Its parishioners are Pimas. It has only one dependent mission: Nuri, six leagues to the east-northeast. The real of SS [Santísima] Trinidad is twelve leagues in the same direction; the real of Río Chico is four leagues west, and the real of Cedros lies six leagues south. The Onabas Mission lies nine leagues to the northwest. [Its minister had to be able to speak more than one tribal dialect.]

Onabas is at 28 degrees, 20 minutes latitude and 266 degrees longitude. It is a principal mission looked after by Father Enrique Kurtzel; his Indians are Pimas. There are two dependent stations: Tónichi five leagues to the north and Soyopa fourteen leagues to the

[3] This is Father José Cabrera Roldán, S.J.

northwest. In both of these, Pimas and Eudebes live intermingled. The reales de minas in the vicinity are Río Chico five leagues south, San Antonio two leagues west of Tónichi, and San Francisco de Asís seven leagues northwest of Onabas. The latter two as well as Soyopa are in the province of Sonora and located on the west bank of the Río Grande.

Cumuripa, at 27 degrees, 45 minutes latitude and 265 degrees, 28 minutes longitude, with its dependent mission of Buenavista is eleven leagues to the south with Father Benito Antonio Romeo, S.J., in charge. Cócorim, the first Yaqui pueblo, lies ten leagues south of Buenavista.

Tecoripa, at 28 degrees, 40 minutes latitude and 264 degrees, 56 minutes longitude, is twenty leagues northwest of Cumuripa and has Father Francisco Javier González in charge. It is a Pima [Baja] mission with two dependent missions: Suaqui ten leagues to the southeast midway on the road from Cumuripa, and San José de Pimas sixteen leagues west of Tecoripa.

Mátape* is a principal mission under the direction of Father Jacobo Sedelmayr at 29 degrees, 20 minutes latitude and 265 degrees, 8 minutes longitude and is twenty leagues north of Tecoripa. Its parishioners are Pimas, Eudebes, and Jovas. It has two dependent missions: Nácori two leagues to the southwest and Alamos seven leagues to the northwest. [It was at Mátape that the first Negro slaves were brought into the Sonora province in 1672–73 by Daniel Angelo Marras, S.J.]

---

* Of Mátape, Polzer writes: "San José de Mátape, situated at the headwaters of the Río Mátape in central Sonora, never enjoyed the prominence of being one of the major Indian centers in the Jesuit mission system of northwestern New Spain. From the time of the first recorded visit to the village in 1622 to the final gathering of the exiled Sonoran Jesuits in 1767, the mission's importance fluctuated with the fortunes of Indian inhabitants and shifts in Jesuit strategy for the conversion of the north.... it was the earliest Sonora mission to be designated a *collegium inchoatum* (incipient college), a status it maintained throughout the greater part of its history." *The Jesuit Mission ...*, p. 129. Also, note 20, p. 141, contains Ortíz Zapata's description of the church edifice at Mátape.

SECTION TWO

The Rectorship of Santos Mártires del Japón

Batuc, an Eudebe settlement and main mission ten leagues east of Mátape and eighteen leagues southeast of Ures over mountainous terrain, is in the charge of Father Alejandro Rapicani. Its geographical position is 29 degrees, 21 minutes latitude and 265 degrees, 38 minutes longitude. It has a beautiful church of hewn stone with a vaulted roof. Its dependent mission, Tepuspe two leagues south, has an almost completed parsonage which is also made of hewn stone. Traveling northward for five leagues, we pass the real of Todos Santos on our right with Carrizal four leagues beyond. Twenty leagues farther, we enter the Tepache Valley with its settlement of Spaniards and Eudebe Indians. Ten leagues still farther we reach Oposura.

Oposura is the main mission where Father Visitor José Garrucho, S.J., with his hospitality will make us forget the weariness of the long journey. The geographical location of this mission is 30 degrees, 50 minutes latitude by 265 degrees, 54 minutes longitude. Populated by Opata Indians and quite a number of Spaniards, it has two dependent missions: Térapa which we passed five leagues before we reached Oposura, and Cumpas eight leagues north of Oposura. In this mission as well as in the adjacent villages of Pívipa one and a half leagues south, Jécori five leagues north, Jamaica two leagues beyond, and the real of Nacozari eighteen leagues north; besides the rather small number of Opata Indians, there are quite a few Spaniards.

After leaving Oposura, we will travel due east five leagues to Tonibabi where we will spend the night so that the seventeen-league journey east to Huásabas will seem shorter. Twelve leagues of this journey are through mountains full of ravines and canyons. We ought to cover these at dawn to avoid the heat of the midday sun which is quite hot in all seasons.

Huásabas is a main mission with Father Juan Nentvig in charge who is also rector of this group of missions. San Ignacio de Oputo, the dependent mission, lies ten leagues to the north. Both are peopled by Opatas and have in their neighborhood numerous deserted mines, such as San Cristóbal five leagues to the east and San Patricio at nearly the same distance to the west. Toward the north, three leagues away, is the abandoned mining settlement of Nori, and nine leagues beyond is San Juan del Río. The village of Guachinera lies fourteen leagues northeast, and the mining settlement of Nacozari fourteen leagues to the northwest. The Fronteras presidio is twenty leagues north-northwest of Oputo.

Once at Huásabas it is necessary to remain a few days to rest, recuperate, and brace ourselves for the eight-league trek to Bacadéhuachi during which a fellow missionary feels obliged to commend himself to Saint Ignatius while climbing and descending such mountain passes replete with declivities and precipices the likes of which he had never encountered in one stretch, not even in the Tarahumara. For this reason and because no one has written about the Huásabas Mission and its dependent mission, we shall proceed leisurely and calmly so that we may become acquainted with it in spite of the discomfort of the minister's house of which a predecessor used to say *Jam non mihi superest sepulchrum.*[4]

After we visit the new church,[5] among the best in Sonora and dedicated to the Apostle of the Indies, St. Francis Javier, let us take our bearings: 30 degrees, 55 minutes latitude and 266 degrees, 15 minutes longitude. When one looks around and is not able to see much of the sky, onc is apt to ask, "What earthly hole have I gotten into?" It is a reasonable question, for this valley on the right bank of the Río Grande[6] is less than a quarter of a league wide. It is between two high and rugged mountains with the river and valley stretching north and south and the eastern mountain less than a quarter of a league away, so jagged and craggy that it reveals no passes except the one southeast leading to Bacadéhuachi and another to the northeast named Cuesta de Tablillas[7] on the road to Guachinera, twenty leagues away.

To the west, at a distance of two leagues filled with hills, gulches,

[4] "The only place left for me to see is my grave."

[5] The Huásabas church was reconstructed by Father Nentvig, who also furnished it with new ornaments.

[6] The Río Grande, as stated in an earlier section, becomes the Yaqui.

[7] In Spanish, cuesta is slope, and tablillas is the plural of mesa in the diminutive form, meaning small, high plateau.

and cuts, there is another mountain; its northern portion is covered with the pine trees we passed on our left when we came from Tonibabi, avoiding the highest and most difficult part of the mountain. South of the same road, the mountain extends for many leagues, almost reaching the Yaqui River. The road is not so lofty, and there are no pine trees, but it is so twisty that the compass needle pivots in all directions as if one were sailing into the wind with the bowline free. For this reason the twisting road is called culebrilla.[8] We must follow it because it affords a less difficult passage, but in so doing, instead of seven or eight leagues from Tonibabi to Huásabas we actually travel twelve. But this applies to all Sonoran roads.

However, the difficult terrain is not so wearisome as one's fear of the Apaches who take cover in these mountains and make forays deeper into the province as they did in the early part of June, 1761, wreaking havoc in Bacanora, San Lucas, Carrizal, etc., when on this same road twenty-five adult Apaches met by mere chance twenty natives of Huásabas; twelve of whom were experienced men and eight were immature boys. After fighting all afternoon, our men sustained four wounded and one dead while the enemy had at least two mortally wounded. The Apaches finally fled from the field, chagrined that a smaller number should have routed their superior forces. Such risks prevail on all roads in Sonora, and it is not safe to travel without escort for which the poor natives are imposed upon, most of the time without pay, because the travelers are so poor they are in need of alms for their own subsistence.

The irrigation of the valley is effected with waters from the Río Grande at a cost of infinite labor. Because its downhill current is so swift, once or twice a year it breaks the dams, and in order to save the crops, it is necessary to rebuild them with incredible zeal. As a rule, sowing is done on the higher fields, and to irrigate those higher fields it is necessary to divert the course of the river one league above and north of Huásabas by means of a costly canal which is in frequent need of repair because of the overflowing creeks that come down from the mountain during the rainy season and break it.

---

[8] Culebrilla means snaky.

Another inconvenience which is no small matter for this mission and its dependent mission is the inconstancy of the river. When winter rains, called quipatas[9] in this region, are not abundant, the river loses its flow by early May, and the wheat crop, without irrigation for a month, either withers or is scanty. These fields are not only suitable for wheat but also for peas, lima and pink beans, and other vegetables. It is not good for corn because the yield does not pay for the work involved.

At both pueblos, Huásabas and Oputo, many fruits grow: figs, cling and freestone peaches, apricots, pomegranates, and quinces. There are also two vineyards, one smaller than the other, which with warm weather and plenty of water grow and produce fine crops, but lacking water, the vineyards dry up and the crops wither. Figs and pomegranates survive the lack of water best.

To the south with a slight westward inclination at a distance of twelve leagues on the road to Tepache four leagues beyond in the same direction, the Huásabas Mission has an excellent farm, the Alamo, with good food-producing land and grazing and watering places throughout, suitable for breeding horses and cattle. It is depopulated at present because of the Apache menace. Even on the river meadows and nearby hills, somewhat distant from this mission, the good grazing fields for all kinds of stock are of little or no use since the horseherd is corralled every night—for what stays out runs the risk of not being there in the morning. Also cattle raising is uncertain because of the many tigers, lions, and wolves that the rugged country shelters. As well as the wild animals, we have the Apache forays, either coming or going. They seize the nearest and tamest, principally at the estancia of Oputo, killing many for food and making shields from the hides.

The dependent mission of San Ignacio de Oputo is located ten leagues north on the right bank of the Río Grande and is much exposed to the incursions of the Apaches. Its soil is better than that of the main mission of Huásabas, yielding besides the products already mentioned, corn, 300 fanegas for one of seed, and wheat, twenty-five to

---

[9] Quipatas is a word used frequently by Father Kino for winter rains. It has become equipatas in modern Spanish.

thirty for one. Of the former, less than one fanega is sown for the mission, and of the latter, eight to ten fanegas of seed are planted for the two pueblos, Huásabas and Oputo. More extensive food-producing fields are available that remain untilled because of the scarcity of natives to work them, difficulties with dams, irrigation canals, and the Apache menace.

For similar reasons the mission had to abandon a beautiful truck-farm watered by a spring. This truck-farm was located half a league west of Oputo at the foot of a mountain and kept the mission supplied with greens, legumes, and various fruits throughout the year.

In the vicinity of Oputo there are many silver mines which are abandoned because of the many outrages committed by the Apaches, such as what happened at Nori, three leagues north of Oputo, and at San Juan del Río, nine leagues beyond in the same direction. Numerous veins with good metal showings have been located southeast, southwest, and northwest of Oputo at distances of from four to fifteen leagues. The color of the mass as well as the night flashes visible during the rainy season are indicative of mineral deposits, but the utter poverty of the residents and the constant enemy danger hamper their being worked. Similar flashes occur in the environs of Huásabas, and the deposits remain untouched for the same reasons. Two rich mines that had been very productive when the Apaches were not coming in so large numbers or so often are now abandoned. One is the San Cristóbal, five leagues to the southwest near the Culebrilla Pass in the vicinity of Tonibabi and within sight of the road. Although it was not easily worked because of the hardness of the rock, it used to yield, and would yet, about half silver. The other mine, the San Patricio, an equal distance to the west, is also idle.

Talk persists among the natives that in the neighborhood of the Culebrilla Pass there is a deposit of virgin silver from which an old man dug up what he needed. He carried no mining tools, only a chopping knife to cut off the portion that he deemed sufficient to cover his immediate needs. Then he melted the mass into slugs in order to disguise the richness of the ore. The old man was accompanied by a boy who served as a sentry to warn of the approach of anyone by throwing a rock, but the old man left the boy at a point where the location of the deposit could not be seen. It has not been possible to learn the location of the deposit from either the old man or the boy.

Another such silver deposit is said to exist on the skirts of the eastern mountain opposite and within sight of the Huásabas Mission. It was thought that the exact location was known to an Indian who died in 1760. However, there is a belief among the natives that he who reveals the site of a mine will soon die. Therefore, a native will not show a mine to a Spaniard for any price, regardless of how advantageous it may be to him, the native, even if the missionary pledges the fulfillment of promises made and the assurance that his life will not be shortened but the Almighty will prolong it if he has the courage to ignore a superstition more fit for old women than brave, sensible men.

The Indian who died in 1760 was half persuaded to show a Spaniard the location of a vein so abounding in silver that the sample he brought flattened when pounded, but while on the way, the Indian must have changed his mind, because when they reached the spot where the sample had supposedly been found, there was no sign of such a vein. After digging all over the hill and finding nothing but dead earth, the Spaniard realized he had been deceived and gave up the search.

During the last two years placer gold has been found on the right bank of the Río Grande in three different locations not far from Oputo, but the nuggets were small. Also, the natives are inexperienced at washing the alluvial deposits and unwilling to do so. Rather, they are fonder of roaming about than seeking wealth. They depart for distant places and return poorer after many days away, and by then their scanty crops have been lost. Richer placers producing larger flakes or grains have been found in the vicinity of El Alamo north of Tepache, and although the residents of Tepache have wealth so close at hand, they prefer to subsist on roots and wild fruits rather than travel three or four leagues to obtain the means to live not only decently but lavishly.

Five leagues north of Huásabas and slightly more than a gunshot east of the road to Oputo there is a vein-like deposit over six yards wide that encircles the base of a small hill which runs from north to south on the eastern side. This vein produces round, stone objects that vary in size from a hen's egg to a cocoanut. The stones are red streaked with white veins and resemble jasper[10] in the rough. Many stones are loose on the surface of the ground; others are entirely submerged. Some of the smaller ones are in clusters of three, four, and six or even more and attached to one another. All of them, large and small, have a pocket in the center filled with a white somewhat yellowish substance which is almost transparent except for a film that covers it like a coating of turpentine. The substance sometimes becomes detached from the walls of the pocket. When this happens, the stone will rattle when shaken. When opened, the cores in most of them are found crystallized in angular patterns so well united, so resplendent and perfectly finished, one would think they had been made by a lapidary. These crystals are set in a hard, flint-like, pearl-bluish, or purple colored substance, difficult, if not impossible, to detach for experimental purposes without defacing them. It has been said that in the beginning this core was of a consistency similar to the white of an egg, and in 1752 I had in my hands a specimen in which the core had not entirely hardened. But upon exposure to the air, it soon petrified. It is evident that this is a rare and new product of nature which, although it brings no revenue to the royal treasury, could be of interest to investigators who, rising above materialism, *ascensiones in corde suo*[11] would admire and praise the power, wisdom, abundance, and beauty of Him who controls all.

Furthermore, around the Huásabas Mission there are abundant deposits of alum and chalk[12] and two hot springs. One is half a league north, and the other is one and a half leagues west. In Oputo there is a similar hot spring half a league west which contains quantities of red ochre of excellent quality.

The climate of this district is dry, healthy, and moderately hot. During the twelve years I have been here I have not known of a

---

[10] Velasco in his *Noticias estadísticas de Sonora* states that the jasper-like rock referred to was used in the altars and pulpit of the church at Sante Fe, New Mexico.

[11] This is from Psalms 82:6 of the Douay English version of the non-Vulgate: "In his heart he was determined to rise gradually."

[12] As for mineral deposits found in Huásabas, alum was probably feldspar, and chalk might have been lime.

contagious epidemic. The medicinal herbs, roots, etc. produced in this province, particularly anise and wild fruits, are excellent. And pitahayas ripen in Huásabas long before they do anywhere else.

Let us proceed to Bacadéhuachi, eight leagues east of Huásabas over a rough and dangerous road, and pass Bacatehac Hill, strewn with crosses inciting our prayers for the many victims of the Apaches. On our way we will stop under the shade of an evergreen oak while the attendants saddle a fresh relay of horses that will take us to Bacadéhuachi, and we shall strive to reach there early.

The main mission of Bacadéhuachi lies at 30 degrees, 53 minutes latitude, 266 degrees, 46 minutes longitude and has two dependent missions: Nácori[13] ten leagues east, and Mochopa[14] two leagues further in the same direction. Father Manuel Aguirre is in charge of the mission, and its inhabitants are Tarahumara and Jova Indians.

The Tarahumara ranch of Sátechi twelve leagues farther away is also under the jurisdiction of Bacadéhuachi. Twelve leagues beyond in the depopulated town of Guainopa there used to be rich silver mines that were worked by a few Spaniards. Another silver mine with its own smelter existed about three leagues northeast of Bacadéhuachi.

Upon arriving, we shall hail the Blessed Madonna of Loreto, the patron saint of this mission. We will then have dinner and a cup of chocolate, as he who arrives late will find nothing to eat, even if he were the father provincial.

There is a hill of rock salt about a quarter of a league east. Just below this hill there is a spring which churns the salt into a foam as white as snowflakes.[15] On our way to the spring we see a hot spring which runs into Bacadéhuachi right through the kitchen of the mission, an advantage not found in any other place in Sonora.

From Bacadéhuachi to the next mission is twenty leagues. We will break up the journey and sleep on the slopes of Guépari Hill eight leagues away so that we may reach our destination by noon the next day.

---

[13] In Opata, *nácori* means "place of prickly pears."

[14] In Opata, *mochopa* means "where black ants dwell."

[15] This rock salt is mentioned in chapter iv, section two.

The Guachinera Mission lies fourteen leagues away from Oputo in a northeasterly direction, and the real de minas of Nacozari is fourteen leagues away to the northwest. The Fronteras presidio is twenty-six leagues to the northwest.

Guachinera, so named because of the abundance of tascal wood[16] found there, is a dependent mission of Bacerac. From Guachinera to a point five leagues north the road is good, but it is kept hot by the Apaches. In the afternoon we will pass by the estancia of Tamichopa, so-called because of the plentiful chamizos[17] that grow in the meadows beside the river.[18]

After crossing the brook a number of times and after having made many turns in the road, we reach Bacerac,[19] the principal mission of this district which is attended by Father José Och. Its geographical location is 32 degrees latitude by 267 degrees, 10 minutes longitude. There are no villages or reales de minas in the vicinity.

Five leagues north on the left bank of the river is the village and mission of Bavispe which is attended temporarily since last March by Father Och.[20] Bavispe is located at 32 degrees, 9 minutes latitude and 267 degrees, 10 minutes longitude.

Proceeding north three more leagues, one reaches the slopes of

---

[16] According to Molina, guachinera in Opata means "place where willow trees abound." Nentvig's reference to tascal is puzzling here. What he refers to may be sabino or ahuehuete: *Taxodium mucronatum,* which is derived from the Aztec *tlaxcal,* the Mexican cypress, also known as *Cupressus benthanni* or *C. thurifera.*

[17] Chamizo is also known as cenizo and is of the *chenopodiacea* family, *Atriplex* group: fourwing, saltbush, or shadscale. These provide food and cover for birds and animals and are an important source of forage for range livestock.

[18] Guachinera Brook.

[19] *Bacerac* in Opata means "where the water is seen," meaning that the course of the river through the mountain canyons cannot be seen from the main road.

[20] Because of the great distance from either Huásabas or Bacadéhuachi, the impossibility of crossing the river during the rainy season, and in the event of illness of the missionary, this very populous district was divided in two, each portion in the charge of a minister.

Carretas,[21] made famous by the numerous Apache outrages committed on the lives and property of travelers and traders. At a distance of thirty leagues northeast is the royal presidio of [San Felipe and Santiago de] Janos.

There were some silver mines being worked near Bavispe when the Apaches were not so much the masters of the country. Now, because we are in the adjacent mountains and at the last mission of this rectorate, we see the Apache fires almost every night.

SECTION THREE

The Rectorate of San Francisco Javier

Cuquiárachi [habitat of doves], our destination, lies well over twenty leagues away in a westerly direction through uninhabited territory with an extremely bad road. We shall leave Bavispe early in the morning with a good escort and spend the night with some degree of safety in the Batepito Valley, twelve leagues away on the Bavispe River. In Opata, Batepito means "where the river makes a turn" and that is exactly what happens. Up till now the course of the river has been from south to north, but at Batepito it turns west. We shall still have at least twelve more leagues to travel before we reach Santa Rosa de Corodéhuachi, a royal presidio commonly known as Fronteras, where we shall stop to eat before proceeding in the afternoon to Cuquiárachi, two leagues away, to meet Father Bartolomé Sáenz, its missionary.

The geographical position of this main mission is 32 degrees, 9 minutes latitude by 265 degrees, 52 minutes longitude. Its two dependent stations are Cuchuta, four leagues to the south, and Teuricachi, three or four leagues farther south. The climate of this rectorate is not healthful, and because of the frequent Apache raids, its population is meager. We must leave quite early in the morning if we are to reach Mababi Pass, six leagues west, before daybreak and avoid being seen by the Apache enemy. They make their lair in the Mababi Mountains, the same mountains we are going to enter. Once at the pass, we must

[21] This is now known as Carreta's Pass.

travel six more leagues to Bacoachi, dependent mission of Arizpe where the renowned gold placers are located. These placers have produced nuggets of two, three, and four pounds[22] but are not so productive at present because the prospectors[23] have been frightened away by the death-dealing Apaches.

From Bacoachi we will follow the course of the Sonora River to another dependent mission of Arizpe: Chinapa, eight leagues to the southwest, leaving the real de minas of Basochuca five leagues away to our left and the real of Bacanuchi four leagues away to our right. The Cananea mines are eight leagues to the northwest. Traveling in a southwesterly direction, we will pass the cattle ranch of Guepavérachi which is owned by gente de razón, and three leagues beyond we will reach the main mission of Arizpe which is located on the right bank of the Sonora River at 31 degrees, 30 minutes latitude and 264 degrees, 55 minutes longitude. Its missionary is the Visitor-General Father Carlos de Roxas, with whose gracious permission we may rest a couple of days, and being in a more populated area than that through which we have been traveling, we can move about with less apprehension.

West of Arizpe six or seven leagues is Santa Rosalía, a site that once had very rich gold mines.

Continuing our journey, we enter the abandoned real of Tetoachi[24] three leagues south, and three leagues still farther by a watery road[25] we reach Sinoquipe,[26] a dependent mission of Banámichi[27] which is five leagues south. About halfway between Banámichi and Sinoquipe we pass the abandoned real of Motepore.

---

[22] The weight is given as stated but is probably meant to be grains.

[23] Nentvig actually used the word buscones, meaning pilferers or petty robbers.

[24] Tetoachi, Nuestra Señora de Aranzazú de Tetoachi, is Tercachi on Nentvig's map.

[25] Watery road is the translation of the expression used by Nentvig: "rather by water." At the time of his journey the Sonora River received the waters of the Moya, Motepori, El Oro, and Opodepe creeks and had overflowed.

[26] Sinoquipe in Opata means "snake on the roof," and it is possible that it may have some connection with macapsinos, glass-snakes, dealt with in section six of chapter iii.

[27] Banámichi in Opata means "rescued from the flood," signifying that the inhabitants were moved to a higher plateau during a flood.

Banámichi, the principal mission, is located on the left bank of the Sonora River at 31 degrees, 2 minutes latitude and 264 degrees, 56 minutes longitude and is administered by Father Francisco Javier Villaroya, S.J. Three leagues farther south we pass through Hüépac,[28] also a dependent mission of Banámichi, and about three leagues beyond we pass by the real of Sonora. One league farther brings us to Aconchi,[29] a main mission administered by Father Nicolás Perera, S.J., at 30 degrees, 56 minutes latitude by 264 degrees, 56 minutes longitude. Then we continue our journey in a southerly direction and reach Babiácora[30] four leagues farther on. Three leagues beyond on our left we pass a small place named Concepción, a dwelling place of Spaniards, and still farther down the river we reach the house of Núñez where he and his family and servants reside.

From here the Sonora River turns westward and follows a winding course through mountain cuts and narrows which we must cross and recross more than thirty times, traveling over rocky slopes for more than ten leagues before we reach level ground. Finally we arrive at Ures, the head mission in charge of Father Andrés Michel since the death of Father Felipe Ségesser [September 28, 1761]. Its geographical position is 30 degrees latitude by 264 degrees, 20 minutes longitude. Its dependent mission, Santa Rosalía, is twelve leagues to the southwest. The real of San José de Gracia is seven leagues west, and the deserted real of Antúnez is six leagues northwest. San Miguel de Horcasitas is about ten leagues west of Ures, and Nacameri, the dependent mission of Opodepe, is six leagues northeast of Antúnez. Nacameri is inhabited by Eudebes, while the Indians in Opodepe are Pimas. Opodepe,[31] where we are going out of curiosity, at 30 degrees, 40 minutes latitude and 264 degrees, 3 minutes longitude, is six leagues almost due north of Nacameri.[32] One league north is the real

[28] Hüépac in Opata means "where the valley expands."

[29] Aconchi in Opata means "at the wall" or "wall remains standing."

[30] Babiácora is so named in Opata because of the abundance of the herb babícori found on the river bank.

[31] Opodepe means "plain where there is granadillo." This is hardwood, *Agonandra obtusifolia, Opu* in Opata, as in Oposura, Opodepe, and Oputo.

[32] Both Opodepe and Nacameri are on the east bank of the San Miguel River.

of San José,[33] and two leagues beyond, there used to be a settlement of gente de razón, breeders of cattle. The mission of Opodepe, ministered by the Rector Francisco Loaiza, has silver and gold mines within its district, the latter having the reputation of producing ore with the highest fineness, and I have seen a piece of gold without rocky mixture weighing seven ounces.

Cucurpe, the last principal mission of this rectorate, is to be our immediate destination. Traveling north from Opodepe seven leagues, we shall enter Toape,[34] an Opata dependent mission of Cucurpe. Six leagues northwest of Toape at 31 degrees, 12 minutes latitude and 263 degrees, 56 minutes longitude, we find the Eudebe Indian mission of Cucurpe, administered by Father Ignacio Pfefferkorn, S. J.

Shortly after leaving Toape, we pass the San Javier ranch on the right bank of the San Miguel River. Four or five leagues east of Cucurpe is the scarcely populated settlement of Eudebe Indians known as Saracachi.[35]

SECTION FOUR
The Rectorate of Pimería Alta (Nuestra Señora de los Dolores)

Dolores, six leagues north of Cucurpe, was the first mission established in this rectorate. Today, with only a few resident Spaniards, it is abandoned as a mission. Formerly its dependent mission, Remedios, four leagues farther north, is now also desolate. Seven leagues farther in the same direction, we encounter Cocóspera, Coespan[36] in Pima, which is twelve leagues directly south of the main mission of Santa María Soamca, under which all three of the afore mentioned missions are now dependent stations.

Santa María Soamca[37] is located at 32 degrees, 28 minutes latitude by 263 degrees, 58 minutes longitude and is attended by Father Diego Barrera with whose permission we shall stir up the fire to prevent our being frozen tonight because the house is exposed to the penetrating

---

[33] This is on the west bank of the San Miguel River.

[34] This is a dependent mission of Cucurpe.

[35] Saracachi in Opata means "metal place."

[36] Coespan in Pima means "a dog's place."

[37] Soamca in Pima means "pure" or "immaculate."

winds that blow the year around. The royal presidio of Terrenate is five leagues to the east, and the valley of San Luis is six leagues to the southwest with the principal mission of Guebavi twelve leagues farther west; Sonoitac[38] is almost ten leagues to the northwest.

From Sonoitac we shall continue our journey to San Xavier del Bac thirty leagues away. Its geographical location is 33 degrees, 52 minutes latitude by 263 degrees longitude. To the west is the sterile wilderness of the Papagos, while to the east is the fertile valley of the Sobahipuris. Casas Grandes, on the Gila, is thirty leagues north, while only three leagues north of San Xavier del Bac is Tucson at 34 degrees latitude, a mission with all the conveniences and many Indians.

Tucson is administered, temporarily, by Father Alonso de Espinosa, S.J., of San Xavier del Bac. Having an excessive number of Indians in his mission, more than any other, Father Espinosa needs another missionary to help keep the older converts in line and to see that the younger Indians he has taught will not lose the faith so that the time he has spent teaching them will not have been wasted. The Pimas of his mission when urged to be obedient reply, "Maybe you think we are Papagos?"[39]

From Tucson we must trek thirty leagues south to reach the royal presidio of Tubac where we can rest and then proceed to Tumacacori, one league south, and then to Calabazas;[40] both are dependent missions of Guebavi,[41] the main mission located at 32 degrees, 28 minutes latitude by 263 degrees, 12 minutes longitude. It is administered by Father Custodio Jimeno who is also in charge of the dependent missions. These are Sonoitac, ten leagues to the northeast; Calabazas, four leagues to the north; and Tumacacori, seven leagues to the northwest. There was a fourth mission: Aribaca, twelve leagues to the northwest, that was destroyed in the 1751 uprising. There are several silver mines and one gold mine in the vicinity of Guebavi, but they are not being worked.

---

[38] Sonoitac is a dependent mission of Guebavi.

[39] By inference this remark has reference to the wildness of the Papagos. They could not be induced to settle in communities and receive instruction.

[40] Calabazas is some distance east of Tumacacori.

[41] The word guebavi is derived from the Pima word *gussuduc,* which means "large body of water." The Santa Cruz River passes through Guebavi.

Resuming our journey, we must travel ten leagues south of Guebavi over mountainous roads before we pass Las Bolas,[42] and two leagues beyond we find the old real of Agua Caliente, only scarcely populated at present. It, too, was destroyed in 1751, and several of its residents were killed.

From here we must travel five leagues southwest to pass through Bussani and then two more leagues to enter Sáric, its head mission. Sáric is under the protection of Our Lady of Sorrows[43] and is located at 31 degrees, 56 minutes latitude by 262 degrees, 58 minutes longitude. It is administered by Father Miguel Gerstner, S.J., who also has charge of the visiting stations of Bisani, two leagues to the north; Arizonac, about half a league northeast of Agua Caliente; and Aquimuri, two leagues east. It was at Sáric that the rebellious Pimas killed eight Spaniards and an equal number of women and children the night of November 20, 1751. Its missionary[44] was forewarned half an hour before the attack and escaped to Tubutama, nine leagues to the south.

Tubutama, a head mission at 31 degrees, 36 minutes latitude and 262 degrees, 56 minutes longitude, is in the charge of the Jesuit Luis Vivas who also attends the dependent mission of Santa Teresa, two leagues to the southwest. It was at Tubutama where fathers Nentvig and Sedelmayr remained besieged for two days and nights. Three of their followers were killed, and eleven more were wounded during the insurrection of 1751.[45]

From Santa Teresa we proceed to Atí,[46] a main mission at 31

---

[42] Las Bolas is also known as Planchas de Plata.

[43] Nuestra Señora de los Dolores.

[44] Father Juan Nentvig, S. J.

[45] There are several excellent accounts of that episode: "Convite evangélico" by Father Salvador Ignacio de la Peña, S.J.; "The Pima Uprising of 1751" by Ewing; *La obra* **II,** pp. 441–2 by Decorme; *Documentos para la historia de México,* fourth series, **I,** pp. 26–76.

[46] The translators have used the most widely accepted spellings of names and places. One may become uncertain whether there are different towns or merely variant spellings of the same town. An example of this may be found by examining San Francisco del Atil, Santa Teresa de Adid, and Santa Rosa de Atí. Roca, in *Paths of the Padres Through Sonora,* sheds some light on the problem (pp. 107–9 and footnote 120, p. 380).

degrees, 27 minutes latitude and 262 degrees, 33 minutes longitude. Because of the death of its minister, Father José Haffenrichter,[47] the mission is in the temporary charge of Father Luis Vivas who also takes care of its dependent mission of Oquitoa, three leagues to the southwest, and, within his capabilities, the mission of San Miguel de Sonoitac, fifty leagues to the northwest. It was at San Miguel de Sonoitac, where Father Enrique Ruhen met a martyr's death in November, 1751. And it was at Oquitoa where the rebels of 1751 killed a justice of the peace and several Spaniards.

Two leagues southwest of Oquitoa is the royal presidio of Altar, and seven leagues in the same direction is Pitic,[48] a dependent mission of Caborca, the principal mission at 30 degrees, 56 minutes latitude by 261 degrees, 49 minutes longitude. There, the rebellious Pimas put to death Father Francisco J. Saéta in 1695 and Father Tomás Tello in 1751. It is administered by Father Antonio María Benz who also tends the dependent missions of Pitic and Bisani, eight leagues farther to the southwest and about twenty leagues from the sea.[49] Several mines have been worked near Bissani, but for some years there has been a great scarcity of water.

From Arizonac to Bissani we have followed the course of the Altar River. Now we shall change our direction to visit San Ignacio,[50] thirty leagues northeast of Caborca, going first to Ocuca,[51] twelve leagues east, then traveling northeast twelve leagues more to Santa Ana which was well populated prior to the insurrection. From there we go due north for five leagues to the abandoned real of San Lorenzo. Then three leagues farther north we pass through the mission of Santa María Magdalena.

Extending our journey two leagues farther, we enter the principal

---

[47] Father José Haffenrichter, S. J., died March 7, 1762.

[48] This should be Pitiquito. Nentvig's map shows two towns named Pitic. The other, far to the south at about 29 degrees latitude by 263 degrees longitude, is much larger. Throughout this section Nentvig means Pitiquito, the northern town at 31 degrees latitude by 262 degrees longitude. In section five he means the southern Pitic.

[49] The Gulf of California.

[50] San Ignacio de Caburica.

[51] Ocuca was a prosperous farm before the uprising of 1751.

mission of San Ignacio de Caburica at 31 degrees, 30 minutes latitude by 263 degrees, 30 minutes longitude. It is administered by Father Francisco Paver, S.J., who took charge following the death of Father Gaspar Stiger,[52] who attended it for over thirty years. Its dependent missions are Santa María Magdalena and Imuris, four leagues to the north.

To summarize, there are thirty-three missions with seventy-eight pueblos and various ranches remaining inhabited:

	Pueblos	Ranches	Tribal Components	Missions
	4	1	Jovas	3
	27		Opatas and Eudebes	11
	10		Eudebes	4
	14		Pimas Bajos	6
	23		Pimas Altos	9
Totals	78	1		33

San Miguel de Sonoitac Mission and two more missions for the Sobahipuris could be added.

Not one of the missions is, or may be called, the principal headquarters of all the missions, but the one in which the father visitor resides is looked upon by the missionaries as the main mission of the province. The father visitor is appointed by his superiors for a period of three years [his superiors having first requested in writing the choice of each individual missionary].

SECTION FIVE

Depopulated Indian Settlements

Nátora,[53] inhabited by Jovas, was ordered abandoned in 1748 by the Viceroy Conde de Revillagigedo because of the distance and the bad road separating it from Teópari from where it was being adminis-

[52] The death of Father Gaspar Stiger, S. J., has not been found recorded, but the last Jesuit catalogue prepared and signed by the provincial, July 12, 1761, has his name with a cross, indicating he had died.

[53] 29 degrees, 30 minutes latitude by 268 degrees longitude.

tered,[54] and its habitants were moved to Pónida, half a league north of Arivechi, from where they were better attended. In 1752 Teópari and Chamada were transferred to Santo Tomás, about two leagues south of Sahuaripa, from where they were administered.

San Mateo, an Opata settlement which was invaded by Apaches in 1752, had its few habitants moved to Sahuaripa.

Also, Rebeico, a Jova village and dependent mission of Mátape, was abandoned.[55]

Santo Tomás de Servas was an Opata village that was destroyed by Jocomes and Sumas in 1690 and its residents distributed among Nácori Chico, Sahuaripa and San Mateo.

Tamichopa, a small place and estancia southeast of Bacerac, was set afire and destroyed by Apaches the day before Palm Sunday,[56] 1758. Only the chapel was spared. Its few Opata inhabitants were absent; otherwise all of them would have been killed.[57]

Twelve leagues north of Oputo, San Juan del Río,[58] Toapora in Opata, was formerly a dependent mission of Teras and later a rich mining center. It was abandoned because of frequent Apache attacks. The ruins of a small chapel are still visible.

Güepa-Comatzi, which means large cave in Opata,[59] was a ranch-village three leagues north of San Juan del Río with very good soil. There was another ranch of the same name twelve leagues south of Bacadéhuachi where large numbers of horses and mules were bred. It was also abandoned because of the Apaches.

Teras, an Opata village intermingled with many Sumas and

---

[54] There is some confusion concerning Teópari. In section one Father Nentvig states it is a dependent mission of Sahuaripa, but here he describes it as a main mission with Nátora its dependent station. *Boletín del Archivo General de la Nación* **XVI,** 4:599–600 declares Teópari was a main mission before 1730 with Santa María de los Dolores its dependent station.

[55] About 1752.

[56] March 18.

[57] In section two of this chapter Father Nentvig gives the impression that Tamichopa was not deserted but served as an estancia, most likely attended by Opatas. The fact that the church edifice was not destroyed suggests that the inhabitants might have taken refuge there and used it as a fortress.

[58] 32 degrees latitude by 266 degrees, 30 minutes longitude.

[59] According to Molina it is a large valley.

Jocomes and formerly a mission, is four leagues south of Güepa-Comatzi. Teras was administered by Franciscan fathers until the Jocomes, Sumas, and some Apaches, dissatisfied with a mulatto steward, opened hostilities against all these pueblos. The missionary had been forewarned and took refuge in Bavispe while the Opata Indians fled, some to Oputo and others to Teuricachi.[60] Teras has ample lands irrigated by canals. All that is needed to make use of them is the repairing of the dams.

At this point I am obliged to state that for the progress of this province it is necessary to promote development of large towns at its frontier valleys such as Teras which could maintain a large community. Other frontier valleys which could accommodate large communities are Batepito,[61] San Bernardino,[62] San Miguel,[63] and Santa Lucía[64] near the source of the Gila River. Also, a large community could exist at Todos Santos on the road to Acome. This plan could be continued to the west along the course of the Gila on its fertile meadows all the way to its junction with the San Pedro River.

If this plan were carried out, the Apaches, who have had free access through that area, would find themselves encircled and would be compelled to submit to the rule of his majesty the king or be annihilated. It would be a great help to repeople the Suma town of Carretas.[65] Good land, water, and a colder climate are found there. Also, it would be well to repeople the Santa Rosa de Corodéhuachi

---

[60] Franciscans were in the area of Bavispe until 1653, but Jesuits gradually replaced them. Indian discontent became apparent as early as 1680, but it was not until 1684 that the Apaches, Jocomes, and Sumas rose in open revolt, which lasted until 1705. The minister referred to was Juan Antonio Estrella, S.J., who, being warned, took refuge in Bavispe. Cf. Spicer's *Cycles of Conquest,* pp. 232–5, and Navarro García's *Sonora y Sinaloa* . . . , pp. 309–17.

[61] Eight leagues north of Teras, Batepito is at 31 degrees, 30 minutes latitude by 266 degrees, 40 minutes longitude.

[62] Eight leagues north of Batepito.

[63] About ten leagues northeast of Batepito.

[64] About 36 degrees latitude by 268 degrees longitude, northeast of Batepito.

[65] About 1684 Carretas was under Franciscan jurisdiction.

Mission in the vicinity of the royal presidio of Fronteras.[66] If these two places were populated, it would impede the Apache incursions into the province of Sonora from the east as well as the west. In this the Terrenate fort would assist.

While so vast a colonization scheme would present many difficulties, this solution to the problem is a desirable one when one considers it would prevent the imminent ruin of a rich province where the royal fifth taxation upon the gold and silver would compensate for the expense incurred in a few years *cum fenore*.[67] If established, this plan would save his majesty 100,000 pesos yearly which is now being spent on the presidios with such meager results.

San José de Guaymas was the only ranchería of the Opan-Guaymas nation.[68] It was created as a mission in 1751 but had to be abandoned by 1759 or '60 because of the scarcity and bad quality of its water and because of the Seri menace.[69] The ranchería was moved farther up the Gulf of California coast closer to Cerro Prieto, near a bay called San Javier that could offer shelter to a whole navy and would favor trade with the Philippines and Peru. The water problem could be overcome by means of cisterns as in Cádiz or by bringing water from the Yaqui River, which is not far away. Most of the former inhabitants are now in Belem, and the rest are scattered in different mining settlements.

Although never a mission, Santa Rosa de Pimas was a ranchería of Pimas Bajos with over 120 families. It was abandoned in 1755 by order of Governor Juan de Mendoza because of the lack of good farming

---

[66] The Santa Rosa de Corodéhuachi Valley gave its name to the mission which was abandoned about 1752 and to the fort, which was more commonly referred to as Fronteras.

[67] Plus a great deal more. Literally: with largess.

[68] The Guaymas Indians are mentioned more fully in chapter v, section one.

[69] Three times before, San José de Guaymas had been used as a mission site: during March and April of 1701 under fathers Salvatierra and Ugarte, during 1704 and 1705 under Francisco María Píccolo, and in 1709 under fathers Juan María Basaldúa and Juan de Ugarte (*Memorias Academia Mexicana de la Historia* **XXVIII**, 2:145–61, 1969).

land. Its inhabitants, who sustained themselves with wild seeds and fruits, were transferred to Suaqui, a dependent mission of Tecoripa.[70]

San José de Pimas, a dependent mission of Tecoripa, was created about 1735 when the now deceased Father Felipe Ségesser joined together two ranches: the San Marcial[71] and the San Lorenzo.[72]

Pitic de Pimas is a very old settlement which shows little or no change from what it was in the beginning. While I know nothing about it, it would seem advisable to move the pueblo down the river to the Hacienda del Pitic, where Governor Agustín Vildósola has established a presidio. The inhabitants of Pitic de Pimas are there now and work as laborers when they feel like it. Otherwise they roam about paying no attention to the cultivation and maintenance of the land and think less of going to confession, even on their deathbeds. They are not in the charge of any priest.

San Francisco [de Pimas] was ten or twelve leagues northeast of Pitic and two or three west of San José de Gracia. It was deserted a good many years before the Seri insurrection.[73]

Nuestra Señora del Pópulo was about half a league northeast of San Miguel.[74] El Pópulo and the village of Los Angeles, its dependent mission a short distance to the southwest, have remained deserted since 1751 when Governor Diego Ortiz Parrilla deported their inhabitants to Mexico and Guatemala.

Mototicachi,[75] in the Pimería Alta between Bacoachi and Terrenate, has been deserted since 1730 because of Apache raids. Its inhabitants left very fertile fields capable of producing much wheat and were moved to Soamca and Cocóspera.

---

[70] Tecoripa was depopulated for a time by Governor Agustín Vildósola for its participation in the Yaqui uprising of 1740–41.

[71] Eight leagues north of Santa Rosa de Pimas and sixteen leagues west of Tecoripa.

[72] Not on Nentvig's map, it is ten leagues northeast of Santa Rosa and six leagues southwest of Tecoripa.

[73] This could have been either 1725 or 1751.

[74] Governor Ortiz Parrilla had assigned extensive communal lands to both San Miguel de Horcasitas and Cerro Pelón, half a league to the south.

[75] 32 degrees, 10 minutes latitude by 262 degrees, 20 minutes longitude.

Nuestra Señora de los Dolores was the first mission established in the Pimería Alta. It was designed and maintained by the virtuous conqueror of the northwest but given up as a mission soon after the establishment of Soamca because of the severity of its climate, which was rapidly causing the death of its inhabitants. With the permission of its vice-patron the lands were sold to Spaniards who still live there in small numbers.

Nuestra Señora de los Remedios was a dependent mission of Dolores and, like Dolores, was deserted because of its climate; its inhabitants were moved to Cocóspera, a dependent mission of Soamca, and the church's ornaments and accessories were taken to Soamca with the understanding that they would be kept there until a mission could be established among the Sobahipuris, something that has not yet been done.

Planned and visited by Father Kino, San Miguel de Sonoitac was established among the Papagos fifty leagues away from the nearest missions: Caborca to the south and Sáric to the east. Since the death in 1751 of Father Enrique Ruhen, its missionary, Sonoitac has remained deserted. Despite the charges against him that were listened to and believed by the murderous, sacrilegious savages, Father Ruhen was an angel, as we who knew him can testify.

Aribaca,[76] destroyed in 1751, was an estancia and dependent mission of Guebavi. Two ranches nearby, Sopori[77] and Tucubavi,[78] have remained deserted although the missionary of Guebavi has sent some cattle there, and the mines in the vicinity are being worked. Two farms near Ocuca[79] have also remained deserted.

But let us leave this subject of depopulated places and gladden our hearts with the churches and missions.

---

[76] 32 degrees, 30 minutes latitude by 262 degrees, 30 minutes longitude.

[77] Northeast of Guebavi.

[78] Southwest of Guebavi.

[79] These farms were far to the south on the Santa Ana River between Santa Ana pueblo and Caborca, near the Picacho Mountains on Nentvig's map at 30 degrees, 30 minutes latitude by 262 degrees, 40 minutes longitude.

VIII

The Missions and Government

SECTION ONE

The Missions: Their Churches, Furnishings, Worship, and Teachings

Although in these miserable times opposing opinions have arisen among critics, some praising and others condemning the care and expense of adorning and maintaining the temples with all possible dignity and decency for the reverence due to the Supreme Maker of all creation, I will not enter into a dispute over the subject, but I believe in what Our Mother, the Holy Roman Catholic Church, has always praised, approved, practised, and in a certain fashion glorified in the lives of its Saints. One learns from the lessons of St Ignatius of Loyola, father and founder of the Society of Jesus, when he says in praise of that Holy Patriarch, "*Templorum nitor, catechismi traditio, concionum ac Sacramentorum frequentia ab ipso incrementum accepere.*"[1] I shall say that my heart rejoices with delight, and I feel more inclined to worship and praise Our Lord when I enter any well adorned church. I must let the admiration argument prevail, *a maiori ad minorem* [from the highest to the lowest], for if we who are more rational than the Indians find incentive and devotion in temples that outshine others by their glowing adornments and will choose those in preference to the slovenly ones for Mass, Sermon, Confession, and Communion, how much more must the Indians be in need of such stimuli when nothing of

[1] "He promoted the erection of splendid churches, fostered the teaching of catechism, encouraged the attendance of sermons and the reception of sacraments." This is from the sixth lesson of the Roman Breviary for July 31, feast day of St. Ignatius.

what they hear takes hold upon them unless it enters through their eyes with some sort of demonstration of the Supreme Creator about whom the preacher is speaking? So, when they see that the house of God is well ordered, clean, and beautifully adorned, they perceive at once the magnificence of its Owner and Ruler. I praise the missionaries of Sonora for imitating their great Father St. Ignatius.

Making use of their own perseverance and the meager labor of the Indians, the missionaries of Sonora have been able to maintain their churches properly, thanks to the Lord. And this is true in all Sonora and almost all the Pimería Alta. However, there are some visiting stations which up till now have not had the means to be restored after being ruined by time and the rebellious enemies.

Because the churches are constructed of adobe, except the one at Batuc, they are in need of repair continually, and only those who build in Sonora know how costly it is. A certain missionary in need of fifty pine rafters offered to pay 2,500 pesos in silver for them but found no sellers. Since there are stone quarries everywhere, if there were stone masons available to construct arches and vaults, the larger investment would mean a saving in the long run.

All the churches have side altars, appropriate ornaments, and chalices of silver and in three instances of gold. There are other sacred vessels such as ciboriums, monstrances, large and small candlesticks and crosses, and nearly all churches have silver statues of the Virgin, organs, bassoons, oboes, and bells, not only at the principal missions but at the dependent ones as well. There are also choruses of Indian singers, and masses are celebrated nearly every Sunday, on days of obligation and on the principal festival days with vespers the evening before when required. And there are processions and other ceremonies of the Holy Church which are accomplished with all possible dignity in order to present a visual display of the majesty of our Holy Religion to the neophytes so that they may remain impressed with its splendor and be attracted to it. Their disposition *piae affectionis*[2] is to believe through their eyes rather than their ears.

On Sundays and festive days the missionaries preach, using as their subjects the Gospel, the significance of the mass itself, the mys-

[2] Impressionable nature.

teries of the faith, and the sacraments, commandments and precepts of the church. After mass on these days all present, young and old, recite the catechism in their language. On other days the boys and girls recite it twice, the first time after mass in their own tongue, and the second time in the evening in Spanish. The native parish officials, the teachers of catechism, and the missionary if he is not occupied with more urgent matters also participate. During Lent it is necessary to preach more often on the Sacraments of Penitence and Communion. The preacher must insist that these sacraments be recited fittingly and properly, and he must not take it for granted that because he preached on the subject the year before it will still be remembered. This is not the case. These sermons must be repeated every year without fail because in such matters the memories of the natives are exceedingly weak. An old-time missionary of Sonora used to say, "There are no Christians in the world who recite the catechism more often and know it less than these Indians." By teaching the Indians diligently the missionaries succeed in having the Indian children conform to the dictates of the Church. They go to confession and receive communion at Easter. And rarely do any of the Opata adults fail to comply unless it be, occasionally, out of ignorance. Among the Opatas, particularly among the women, there are some who confess and receive communion at other holidays during the year which is a source of gratification for their missionary. In some missions, especially those where the Virgin of Loreto is venerated as in Mátape, Bacoachi, and Oposura, the rosary is recited every night in her chapel even if there is only one parishioner in the church. In other places the catechism is recited for a third time in some home so that all may hear it and have their memories refreshed. In every mission the rosary, the litanies, and Hail Marys are recited on Saturday nights, and in most of them the litanies and Hail Marys are sung with musical accompaniment. The Opatas are so devout that they insist upon hearing mass every Saturday night in spite of their having been told that it is not obligatory.

SECTION TWO

Ecclesiastical and Civil Governments

Let us deal first with the ecclesiastical government. The catechism class must be attended by boys and girls from the age of seven until they are married and have children. At that time they are examined by the missionary, and if found proficient they are excused. The missionary is assisted by one to three fiscales,[3] depending upon the number of inhabitants in the parish. Fiscales are also known as madores. Their duties are to notarize the marriage bans and serve as sextons and grave diggers. The temastianes[4] act as prompters during the catechism and also teach the catechism class. They, too, serve as sextons. If the teacher knows how to read and write music, he will serve as the musical director of both the chorus and band which take part in religious ceremonies and perform chants as well as musical selections.[5] The teacher also serves as scribe for the town council. It is admirable that these illiterate people are able to memorize chants for as many as four different types of masses, the Psalms, and responses for pertinent burial services.

The civil government consists of the governor,[6] the alcalde,[7] the alguacil,[8] and topil.[9] The governor is a native selected by the inhabitants of the pueblo in the presence of the missionary who directs the inhabitants to be sure that the elected man is one who leads a good life thus setting an example that will stimulate and spur them to be good. This is in accord with the laws of September 25, 1716, issued by the Royal Court of Guadalajara and a dispatch of November 25, 1746, from the Viceroy Don Juan Francisco Güemes y Horcasitas which

---

[3] The native parish officials referred to in section one of this chapter were known as fiscales.

[4] The native teachers of catechism referred to in section one were known as temastianes.

[5] Nentvig uses the expressions canto llano and canto figurado. Canto llano meant Gregorian chants or simple music with extremely regular cadences. Canto figurado referred to music with varied rhythms, songs which could be adapted to varying times and different rhymes.

[6] The native governor was usually referred to as gobernadorcillo to distinguish him from the governor of the province.

[7] Alcalde, usually mayor of the town, was actually a justice of the peace in the pueblos. Alcalde Mayor refers to the governor of the whole province.

[8] Alguacil was a sort of constable.

[9] Topil was the lowest native official. He was a combination policeman and caretaker of church property.

contain points of great importance. Would to God that these points be observed to the letter so that thousands of offenses to God, our Lord, might be stopped, and the decline of the pueblos might be prevented. As it is now, the natives leave the pueblos to go to reales de minas with no desire to return. This leaves their wives as widows and their children as orphans.

Once the governor is selected, the people of the pueblo select the justice of the peace, the constable, and the policeman in the same way. Then in the same manner they select their warchief,[10] and all together these elected officials form the senate or council of these republics, maintaining order and safeguarding the property of the king and the church, settling disputes, chastising delinquents, and imposing penalties of one or two dozen lashes according to the crime, especially if it is a public offense. The council regulates what is to be done for the church and has authority over the cultivation of the soil, sowing, reaping, and other occupations in which the natives are supposed to spend three days a week. But actually the Indians work less than a day. For no matter how much the justices may exert themselves to get the Indians out at an early hour, they arrive on the job at noon when the sun is at its zenith. Once there, they do not apply themselves to finish the work but rather play around until three or four in the afternoon. Then, even though the day has been miserably lost, they are well satisfied with what they have done and gorge themselves with pozole, a stew prepared for them containing lima beans, chick-peas, carob beans, wheat, and even meat when available to improve the flavor. The food is obtained from the storerooms of the mission.

When harvesting wheat they receive a whole cow every day, but even though the Indians know and admit that the work they are asked to do is for their own benefit, the justices and the missionary must exert great effort, especially among the Pimas, to prevent the Indians from entirely neglecting to provide for their own sustenance. At times it is necessary for the justices to apply the penalty of a few lashes. This has even been done with the Opatas, reasonable as they seem to be.

The warchief in the smaller settlements has an ensign and a

[10] Capitán de guerra or Capitán a guerra.

sergeant under his command. In the larger pueblos he may also have one or two corporals, etc. Their duty is to reconnoiter in all directions for a distance of two or three leagues from the village looking for enemy tracks. Should any be found, the governor is notified, and he orders out as many warriors as he judges necessary. The warriors, then, are under the command of the warchief. Moreover, the warchief or one of his officers commands the escort that accompanies traders, travelers, and the missionary when he goes on visitations or trips to see fellow missionaries. Furthermore, the warchief furnishes the guard when mission crops are transported to be sold at some mining district. He has no duty in the town.

Lately the rank of captain-general has been introduced, which serves no purpose either to religion, the kingdom, or the public. Such an office did not exist among the natives.[11] They only recognized and obeyed the boldest and most courageous who led them in offensive warfare and scrimmages that occurred among them such as when the people of Bacerac would come by night and steal the salt rock of Bacadéhuachi which was needed as a condiment in their stews because the Baceracas had none. Then the Bacadéhuachis would come out and defend what they claimed was theirs. The captain-general rank is not good for the faith, because no matter how good an Indian might have been before he was shown this esteem, the praise and prestige he receives make him arrogant rather than humble, and lazy rather than diligent. There is nothing more for him to attain. While he had been obedient and gentle, he becomes stubborn and willful, and the worst is that with the honor conferred upon him he turns from being a good Christian to being a bad one. Many examples could be cited, but it is enough to say that Luis de Sáric would never have plotted his insurrection[12] had he not been captain-general of the Pimas Altos.

If a captain-general becomes corrupt, all the vicious and wayward Indians find protection under his shadow and revert to the pagan

---

[11] Governor of Sonora Diego Ortiz Parrilla conferred the honorary title of Captain-General of the Aboriginal Tribes on Luis de Sáric in 1750. While there had been such a rank in the Spanish Army, there had not been such a rank among the aboriginal tribes.

[12] The Pima uprising of 1751.

practices of drunkenness, dances, and orgies. The captain-general avails himself not only of their services but also their possessions. He considers them his inferiors, and while he remains in office, they do not dare open their mouths in the slightest whimper to reveal their suffering, even to their missionary, for the fear they have of such a leader. Therefore, it is evident that such an office is not beneficial to the kingdom. It is contrary to the royal will as prescribed by the Laws of Indies. In case of emergencies the warriors can be gathered quicker by notifying the gobernadorcillos, who can send messengers who travel in relays over great distances. From a far corner of the province, then, the gobernadorcillos can issue one order dispatching the required number of warriors from each pueblo. But if the request goes first to the captain-general, as I have seen many times, he will send many orders, each one prepared very slowly beginning with "I," then the name of the captain-general, "order . . . " This is a hindrance rather than a benefit to the public good. Such an office does not benefit the natives. It is prejudicial to Christianity and the welfare of their souls.

Furthermore, in the Indians' desire to imitate Spanish officers they lose the value and efficiency of their own weapons, disdaining to go on foot and carry bows and arrows. So they demand firearms, horses and the necessary riding gear, but they do not know how to use them.[13] They make themselves utterly useless and ridiculous, and the civil authorities do not try to stop them as prescribed by the Laws of Indies.[14] Thus the number of warriors on foot handling native weapons with proficiency becomes fewer each day. Therefore, it is my opinion that it would be wiser to allow those who hold the office of captain-general to continue serving in that capacity unless they abuse it, but as they die off or prove themselves unworthy, new ones should not be appointed.[15]

---

[13] Here Nentvig gives the impression that the Indians were poor horsemen as well as inefficient with firearms. Actually, the Indians were quite competent in both.

[14] Book **VI**, Title 1, Articles 31 and 33.

[15] Although Nentvig gives the impression that there were many Indians with the rank of captain-general, this was not the case. Only one captain-general served in the province of Sonora.

Although this may not be the proper place, I wish to make reference to the subject of dealing with the Indians. I wish to call to the attention of those who deal with Indians that they should not praise any of them to their faces. To the native it is a poison of a violent kind to hear himself praised and addressed as señor as is often done by incautious Spaniards in order to obtain what they would never acquire without such folly. Not long ago I saw a paper written by a Spaniard who had been a judge for years. He addressed it to a native, and he began with these words, "Señor Gobernador ... " If this style were used by a Negro or a mulatto it wouldn't surprise me because he would be addressing a superior, but it becomes an offense to his noble race for a Spaniard to address an Indian that way. It is a despicable, stupid affront, even more so if it is used as bait to obtain favors.

IX

Settlements

Preamble

As I undertake the writing of this chapter, I cannot see a way to temporize the boredom of my readers unless we change ourselves into spirits and, laying aside the burden of our bodies, survey this province from a suitable height as we did the missions. Otherwise we would have to undertake journeys twice as long with less comfortable lodgings, and a greater scarcity of food and transportation. With this explanation we shall begin our flight . . .

SECTION ONE

Mining Camps and Settlements of Spaniards

Real de la Santísima Trinidad, 28 degrees, 12 minutes latitude, 267 degrees longitude, was founded in 1754 when rich silver deposits were discovered.[1] The mine by itself sustained the province of Ostimuri for five whole years. It is capable of producing much more than it has, but disputes, changes of ownership, and mismanagement have hindered it greatly. Indeed, it is operated wholly in opposition to the existing mining laws. Its yield by the firing process was high and by the mercury[2] process considerably higher. It is now being worked secretly, and the returns with little effort are said to be good. There are

[1] Almada's *Diccionario,* p. 797, gives the date of the discovery of silver in that area as 1740.

[2] Amalgamation.

two small mines in the vicinity also: the Santa Ana to the southeast and the Guadalupe to the southwest.

The real de Río Chico[3] is one of the oldest. It includes the Cobriza mine three leagues away which yields three to six marcos[4] per carga[5] and even a marco per arroba;[6] the La Dura[7] mine with a yield of nine marcos per carga; and the Potrero and Proterillo mines, which are five leagues away, render up to three marcos of silver to the arroba. Río Chico, site of the curacy, has thirty or more residents, and to the south-southwest it has the Luceros ranch six leagues away. The Sauce ranch[8] is one league away, and the Duarte ranch is five leagues distant. And the ranches at Las Animas, García, Carrizal, and Cerro Colorado are three leagues away and deserted now because of the Seris. The last two are dependent on the Onabas Mission.

Tacupeto[9] is a small settlement that offers nothing worth mentioning.

The real of Ostimuri, which gave its name to this province, has been abandoned because its ore veins have run out.

The real of Vatemaneco in the vicinity of Ostimuri was abandoned because of the flooding of its shafts, but the waters have been drawn out of the main shaft, and they have begun to work it again.

The ranches of Carrizal, Milpillas, Vícora, Sapora, and Palmar, all east of Onabas, and the ranch of Techomoa to the south remain inhabited.

Following on from the ranches, we reach the real of San Antonio de la Huerta[10] in the province of Sonora. Here the alcalde mayor

[3] Previously San Miguel Arcángel was the seat of the curacy. By 1684 it had been transferred to San Francisco de Asís de Río Chico.

[4] Marco, or mark, is a unit of weight equal to eight ounces.

[5] Carga, or load, is the amount a beast of burden can carry, 100–150 pounds, depending upon distance and roughness of terrain. In mining terminology a carga was 300 pounds. Ward's *Mexico in 1827* **I**, p. 573.

[6] Arroba is a unit of weight equal to twenty-five pounds.

[7] La Dura, the hard one in Spanish, was so named because of the hardness of the rock in which the ore was imbedded.

[8] Sauce means willow in Spanish.

[9] Tacupeto is north of Trinidad and Onapa.

[10] San Antonio de la Huerta is north of Onavas.

resides and here is most of the commerce in the province even though the placer gold deposits discovered accidentally in 1759 have dwindled considerably. Placer gold was discovered when a servant spilled some quicksilver in a brook, and when he tried to recover it, he noticed minute grains of gold interspersed among the sand of the brook. Since there are occurrences of this nature in so many places in Sonora, in the hills as well as in the sands of the streams, one cannot help but believe that the whole province must be pregnant with the necessary elements needed for the generation and maturation of this precious metal, particularly where stones called tepustete,[11] referred to as the "guide of gold," are found. The tepustete is a very heavy stone on the order of lead ore, and if one digs where it is found, one is apt to uncover gold, but not in all cases, nor in quantities desired by the seeker, that is, handfuls acquired with little effort. So great is the laziness and love of idleness of most of these people that in spite of the abundance of gold in more than twenty different places, most of the people remain poor. They do not persevere at any one place, and when they hear of another spot, they leave what they have to ride the trail of doubtful hopes. They are much like the mastiff that, letting the piece of meat he carried in his mouth drop, ran after its own image reflected in the water.

Turning back on our mental flight and gazing down on San Antonio de la Huerta, we will see the famous canyon extending from Tónichi to Mátape and containing Las Tortugas ranch,[12] the deserted real of San Francisco, the village of Soyopa, and the old mining settlement of Rebeico.[13]

Glancing toward the south and southwest, we see the abandoned real of San Miguel,[14] the oldest real and formerly head of the curacy.

---

[11] Tepustete is a hematite, bloodlike, ferric oxide. Information on tepustete may be found in Bolton's *Anza's California Expeditions* **II**, p. 152, and Sobarzo's *Vocabulario,* pp. 319–20.

[12] Tónichi is to the south, and Mátape lies to the northwest.

[13] San Francisco de Rebeico, founded in 1673.

[14] Although the full name was seldom used, this is San Miguel Arcángel, a mining settlement founded around 1660 and attended by Father Daniel Angelo Marras, S.J., for over seven years; it was in existence until shortly after 1731 and was located between Onavas and Tecoripa.

Now the curacy is at Río Chico. Besides the real of Río Chico, there are the reales of Cosari, Ventana, and Mortero. All of these reales have been abandoned for years for lack of ore.

Then, too, there are the ranches of Sortillones, Aldamas, Santa Barbara, Ciénega, Sauz, Córdova, Canito, Machavavi, and Agua Caliente plus the small real of San Juan Bautista which produces a reasonable yield.

To the west we see the Spanish settlement of Mazatán five leagues west of Mátape. Farther west we see the mining settlements of Quisani, Aigame,[15] the Aguaje,[16] and just beyond we see Las Animas. All four mining settlements have rich mines that yielded bountifully in 1756 and 1757, but they are abandoned at present because of the Seri menace. Also in that direction we see the village of San Cosme and a ranch formerly owned by [the late] Captain Juan Tomás Velderrain.[17] The ranch is now deserted because of the enemy. There are several other ranches where many stray animals that have wandered from flocks and herds have multiplied, but the names of these ranches have escaped my memory.

The San Francisco real has silver-producing mines which are abandoned because its workers were lured by what gold-mining settlements might offer. The workers left, and they who used to support themselves with decency in this locale have returned destitute.

But the sight of a country so unfortunate tires the wings of our fancy, so let us proceed on a short flight of twenty leagues to the north and rest at Cerro Alto, here on the right bank of the Río Grande opposite the real of Todos Santos[18] which has a reduction plant and several bone calcination furnaces which refine the lead-containing ores of the Carrizal mine.[19] At present the mine is not in operation.

---

[15] This is Aguame on Nentvig's map.

[16] Aguaje means running spring in Spanish.

[17] Captain Juan Tomás Velderrain owned three ranches; another is mentioned further on in this section. He was the military commander of Tubac and was married to the daughter of the governor. Velderrain died September 7, 1759.

[18] This is Todos S.S. on Nentvig's map.

[19] The Carrizal mine is five leagues north of Todos Santos.

The Carrizal de Abajo, a league and a half southwest of the Carrizal mine, is also abandoned. Three leagues north of Carrizal de Abajo one finds a ranchería of Pimas, and seven leagues still farther north is the town of La Junta. Both are abandoned.

Looking toward the southeast one finds more deserted places such as Santa Catarina in the neighborhood of Bacanora and the ranches of San Lucas and Sásachi.[20] The Palos Blancos placer mine is two leagues farther east. The real of Guainopa and other abandoned mines are still farther east in the vicinity of the Sátechi ranch.

More to the north, two leagues from Bacadéhuachi, is an abandoned real that used to yield one marco of silver to the arroba from its own smelting plant. Various other mines near Guachinera remain untouched because of the Apaches.

Between Guachinera and Bacerac is Tátzida, an old estancia, and the town of Tamichopa[21] and its estancia. There is also a ranch belonging to the mission of Bacerac and another ranch belonging to the mission of Nácori.[22]

What we discover from our view from Todos Santos toward the west and northwest brings us horror, for there are, almost in a chain, so many ranches and estancias destroyed by the Apaches that I shall be content merely to give their names and approximate locations: The Realito[23] is between Batuc and Mátape. San Jago[24] was a real and later a cattle ranch. Then there is Agua Caliente.[25] Farther on, there is Machacubiri,[26] a ranch owned by the Salmons. These last two and the ones following were destroyed by the Apaches in 1751 and after: Topisco to the north of Mátape, the Solia,[27] the Rodríguez ranch four leagues beyond, Banachari[28] which is the citadel of Mátape, Batasagui four leagues beyond, and the ranch of Ojitos still farther.

---

[20] The ranches are five leagues from Todos Santos.

[21] Tamichopa is a league north of Guachinera.

[22] This is Nácori Chico.

[23] Actually, the Realito is a league north of Batuc.

[24] San Jago is seven leagues northwest of Batuc.

[25] Agua Caliente is also seven leagues northwest of Batuc.

[26] Machacubiri is six leagues west of Batuc.

[27] This is Soliz on Nentvig's map.

[28] Banachari is five leagues northwest of Batuc.

We will take another jump, this time northward to the Sierra Alta between Huásabas and Oposura.[29] Our flight will pass over the small valley of Tepache about one league long with its Opata settlement of Tepache,[30] previously a real[31] with the mines of Arroyo, Nacatovori, Lampazos, Las Guijas, Santo Domingo, and Coronilla in its vicinity. All these mines yielded well but are unworked at present. The still visible ruins are proof of their former grandeur.

Promontorios, San José del Alamo, and Salitral mines are in the neighborhood of Huásabas and only a short distance from one another. The San José del Alamo is a placer mine that has yielded gold nuggets of fair size, and with the Salitral mine is being worked anew.

Tonibabi, a Spanish settlement four or five leagues east of Oposura at the foot of Sierra Alta, is inhabited by thirty-two individuals who, excepting three or four, are very poor, and because of the continuous hostilities of the Apaches, they are unable to work the mines inherited from their ancestors. The mines include the San Patricio, five leagues east, which by smelting rendered one marco per arroba; the San Cristóbal, two leagues to the southeast, which, though the rock was hard, yielded half silver intermittently, the silver being in pockets, and another vein, somewhat deeper, yielded one marco per arroba; the Plomosa, a league away, yielding three marcos per carga, is now flooded.

Skirting the side of the mountain, we find on the right of the road to Huásabas several streaks of lead ore that no one has worked, and near Tonibabi we find three lead mines within a radius of half a league: the Cozinera yielding three marcos to the carga, the San José yielding three to five marcos, and the San Antonio yielding six to nine marcos. There are many more mines but all are abandoned because of the

---

[29] Ca. 31 degrees latitude, 266 degrees longitude.

[30] Nuestra Señora de San Joaquín y Santa Ana de Tepache.

[31] Mines were discovered and worked by Spaniards in 1660. Being a real, it was attended by a diocesan minister, but because of the great distance the minister had to travel, the curate of San Miguel de Horcasitas requested that its spiritual needs be attended to by the Jesuits of Batuc. The importance of this real is shown by the fact that it had two justices of the peace and was the residence of the lieutenant governor. It was visited on January 8, 1686, by mining inspector D. Gabriel de Isturiz, at which time it had 142 families, 388 people.

Apache enemy. The residents sustain themselves with a few cows and small plots of ground left to them which they plant in season.

As for deserted ranches in this vicinity, there are the Moreno's, five leagues to the east almost to the Culebrilla Pass; El Médico, two leagues beyond; and another Moreno ranch in the Capadéhuachi Canyon with good irrigated fields and pasture land suitable for breeding all kinds of livestock.

The old real of San Javier is about five leagues north of Huásabas, west of the Capadéhuachi Canyon, fourteen leagues northeast of Cumpas, and within the mountains. The real of Mololea is three leagues from San Javier and eleven leagues northeast of Cumpas. The San Javier real is five leagues east of Nacozari, and the Mololea real is seven leagues from Nacozari.

Turning our eyes to the southwest, we see the Pivipa settlement six leagues from Tonibabi and one league south of Oposura. The residents of Pivipa support themselves by working their fields and breeding some livestock. To the southwest of Pivipa we see the ranches of Terecomachi, Comaguita, Massocagui, Comatzi, and Navachi. Two leagues farther in the same direction we see the Los Chinos ranch, and beyond that another league we see El Sauce ranch belonging to the Núñez family. All these ranches were abandoned because of the Apache incursions of 1753 and 1754. Going four leagues farther west toward Ures, we see Las Bolas, another Velderrain ranch. And two leagues still farther we find a farm belonging to the Ures Mission. The estancia of Sonibiate, burned down by the Seris in 1755, is seven leagues to the northeast. Las Bolas and the Ures Mission farm were abandoned in 1754 because of the Seri and Apache hostilities.

The small village of Concepción with its Cerro Gordo mines is northeast of Ures four leagues south of Babiácora. And the ruins of the Usabra and Teguatzi ranches lie to the east, four to five leagues west of Pivipa. About one league north of Usabra is the estancia of Pastoría with the Las Lajas ranch to the east. And the settlement of Bacachi with an orchard is two leagues to the northeast. All these places were depopulated in 1753 and 1754.

The real of San Juan Bautista,[32] eight leagues northwest of Oposura, had been the site of a curacy and the capital of Sonora but was

[32] San Juan on Nentvig's map.

abandoned May 3, 1751. The Santa Barbara ranch, owned by Bachelor Juan José de Grijalva,[33] is four leagues east of San Juan and was deserted in 1753. Another Moreno ranch, Los Alamos, four leagues to the southeast, was abandoned in 1748 or 1749. At the same time the settlements of Basura, Badéhuachi, El Destierro, Paquillo, and González were also forsaken. The Munguía ranch a league north of San Juan was attacked and destroyed by the Apaches in 1744. The ranches of Bachelor Soto and Baroyesa northwest of San Juan Bautista real suffered the same fate as did the Durazno and Salazar ranches six leagues and four leagues west of Cumpas respectively. These last two ranches were attacked and destroyed by Apaches February 19, 1743, and forty-four of their residents were killed. Six years before, the Meco ranch and the one owned by Don Antonio de Mendoza, both west of the mountains, met the same disaster. The ranches of Torreón, Tepuchi, Monte Grande, and Santa Rosa, all near Basochuca,[34] were also victims of the enemy.

The small Spanish settlement of Teonadepa is half a league west of Cumpas.[35] The depopulated ranches of Grijalva and Argüelles are farther down the river to the southeast but not so far as Jamaica. The Jamaican mines with their reduction works are the property of Don Julián Moreno and are two leagues south of Cumpas.

Jécori, a mediocre settlement of Spaniards, is two leagues south of Jamaica, and to the southeast about two leagues apart are three abandoned estancias: One is owned by Don Gregorio.[36] Another is the property of Bachelor Juan José de Grijalva, and a third belongs to the Oposura Mission. A deserted mining settlement is also in the vicinity.

The old real of Nacozari[37] is fourteen leagues north of Cumpas. The real had been densely populated and very productive. At present it is inhabited by Don Manuel Vázquez, a few impoverished gente de

---

[33] Bachelor Juan José de Grijalva was a diocesan priest. Bachelor signifies Bachelor of Theology, a degree held by all diocesan priests and curates.

[34] 31 degrees, 40 minutes latitude, 265 degrees, 10 minutes longitude.

[35] Nentvig's map shows Teonadepa to the south of Cumpas.

[36] This is probably Gregorio Alvarez Tuñón Quirós, alcalde mayor of Sonora and wealthy mine owner, who also served as a captain at Fronteras presidio, Almada's *Diccionario*, pp. 58–60.

[37] Established ca. 1660.

razón and some Opatas. Its mines are being worked badly and in a small scale.

Five leagues north of Nacozari is the real of Chunerobabi, which yielded traces of gold and three to four marcos of silver to the arroba. This real and the real of El Aguaje, attacked by Apaches on March 5, 1742, and again in 1744, remain unworked. The gold and silver reales of de la Peña, Nacozari Viejo, Hacienda Vieja, and El Barrigón are all two to four leagues from Nacozari and have been abandoned because of the enemy menace. Other mining properties such as the Huacal, Pinal, Toaportze, Nori, and San Juan del Río, all somewhat distant, have remained idle for the same reason even though their yields were as high as seventy-five marcos of silver per quintal.[38]

The Escalante ranch with its reduction works is one league north of Nacozari. The Corella ranch is one league beyond, and the Cárdenas ranch is still two leagues farther. There are two or three other ranches in the immediate vicinity which are also deserted because of the Apache atrocities.

When we consider that we have seen over eighty deserted ranches, estancias and mining settlements, and scarcely ten inhabited places, who will doubt that Sonora is in danger of perishing?

SECTION TWO

The Royal Presidios and Intermediate Villages

After having wearied our eyes and saddened our minds with so much desolation, we need to take another imaginative flight to visit the five presidios that his majesty maintains at so great an expense for the defense of this unhappy land. This flight is necessary so that we might see the territory, inhabited or deserted, that lies between the forts.

We shall start with the presidio at Fronteras, also known as Santa Rosa de Corodéhuachi,[39] 32 degrees, 10 minutes latitude, 265 degrees, 46 minutes longitude. It was the first and only presidio in Sonora from 1690 to 1740. The Jocomes, Sumas, Janos, and Apaches rose in revolt

---

[38] As given in the notes on chapter vi, a quintal is a unit of weight equal to 100 pounds.

[39] The combined name of Santa Rosa de Corodéhuachi resulted, but the name Fronteras, frontier presidio, sprang up and was in general usage.

in 1686 and attacked Santa Rosa, an Opata village eight leagues north of Cuquiárachi, on May 10, 1688, and Cuquiárachi itself on June 11, 1689, forcing the Opata population to withdraw to Corodéhuachi. The fifteen soldiers from the presidio of Sinaloa who had been stationed at Teuricachi for three years were moved to the beautiful site at Corodéhuachi with its own spring, and when this happened in 1690 or 1691, the Indians were transferred, some to Teuricachi and the rest to Cuquiárachi.

The missions of Cuquiárachi, established in 1660, Santa Rosa and Cuchuta, both established in 1686,[40] and the dependent mission of Teras were more and more frequently the victims of the incursions of the four tribes mentioned for nearly ninety years.

To the northeast in the vicinity of the San Bernardino Valley there are vestiges of settlements that existed so long ago that no living soul remembers them. The names Cuchuvérachi,[41] Batepito,[42] Naideni Bacachi,[43] and Chiricagui[44] are Opata words and would indicate that this was land of the Opata nation.

The presidio of Terrenate is northwest of Fronteras thirty leagues away through the Magallanes Pass.[45] So that we may not omit any point worthy of attention, we will take a look at Basochuca real where a few poor Spaniards are unable to work the several mines in its vicinity. Nacozari is ten leagues east of Basochuca, and four or five leagues north of Basochuca lies Bacoachi with its gold placers.

The abandoned gold real of Santa Rosalía is five or six leagues west of Arizpe, and the deserted mining settlement of Tetoatzi is four leagues south of Arizpe. Two leagues southwest of Tetoatzi is

---

[40] The dates given refer to when missionaries were stationed at each. Actually, Cuquiárachi was established as a Jesuit mission in 1646 by Gerónimo de la Canal but had remained without a missionary from 1653 until 1660 when Antonio de Heredia, S.J., took charge. Cuchuta was established in 1653.

[41] In Opata, Cuchuvérachi means canyon and brook where the matelote fish is found. Matelote is the regional name for róbalo.

[42] In Opata, Batepito means where the river makes a turn.

[43] In Opata, Naideni-Bacachi means land of the beautiful reeds.

[44] This is Chiguicagui on Nentvig's map, 34 degrees, 30 minutes latitude by 265 degrees longitude; cf. chapter iii, section one, footnote 3.

[45] 31 degrees, 40 minutes latitude by 265 degrees, 20 minutes longitude.

Teguatzi, a ranch owned by Don Agustín Vildósola which was attacked by Apaches February 22, 1746. It is depopulated at present.

A short distance north of Arizpe is the real of Bacanuchi, and eight leagues northwest of Bacanuchi is the real of Cananea, entirely deserted this year, 1763. There are a few deserted ranches and estancias between all these places, but I lack the information to distinguish one from another.

Now we arrive at the presidio of Terrenate[46] which was built in 1742 to restrain the Apaches and prevent them from entering the Pimería. However, since the establishment of the presidio, the Apache enemy has caused more destruction in the province of Sonora than ever before.

The main mission of Santa María Soamca is five leagues to the west, and two leagues south of Soamca there is a deserted ranch. The ranch of San Lázaro is one league farther south. Two leagues west of San Lázaro is the Divisaderos ranch, and eight leagues south of that is the ranch-hamlet and estancia of Sicurisudac where the Apaches committed grievous killings and barbarous atrocities in 1730.

Cocóspera is a dependent mission of Soamca twelve leagues southwest of Terrenate. Cocóspera was attacked by Apaches on February 16, 1746, and its church burned down.

The Santa Barbara, Buenavista, and San Luis ranches, close to one another five to eight leagues from Soamca, are deserted.

The main mission of Guebavi is less than three leagues northwest of Buenavista, and the Tubac presidio[47] is seven leagues beyond Buenavista in the same direction. The presidio of Tubac was established in 1752 and occupies the Pima settlement of that name. The Indians were moved to Tumacacori where they lack the good land of Tubac and can only sow seasonally. In the vicinity of this presidio are the depopulated ranches of Sopori somewhat more than two leagues north, Tucubabi thirteen leagues southwest, and Aribaca seven leagues northwest.[48] The village of San Luis Beltrán is thirty leagues to the southwest.

---

[46] Nentvig has jumped northwest from Fronteras to Terrenate, 32 degrees, 40 minutes latitude by 264 degrees, 12 minutes longitude.

[47] 32 degrees, 58 minutes latitude by 263 degrees, 18 minutes longitude.

[48] Aribaca was also an estancia and visiting station.

The Cerro[49] is eighteen leagues south of Tubac. Also south of the presidio is the deserted real of Las Bolas, famed for its prodigious masses of virgin silver. The rich real of Agua Caliente is two leagues farther south; it is not being worked at present. The abandoned real of Sombreretillo lies a short distance west of Sáric, and there was a gold and silver mine one league north of Sáric which had been worked.

The Altar presidio[50] is forty leagues from the Gulf of California and was established in 1753 or 1754 because of the Pima outbreak of 1751. Twenty men of its garrison originally stationed at Sinaloa were transferred to Buenavista in 1741 because of the Yaqui rebellion of 1740, and in 1751 they were sent to the Pimería to help suppress the Pima revolt of that year. When these soldiers were assigned to Altar under the command of Don Bernardo Urrea,[51] the garrison reached its full strength of fifty men, the other thirty troops being newly enlisted men.

Most of what is to be seen in this district has been dealt with in chapter vii, section four, except the following: the depopulated real of Ocuca, a league east of the pueblo of the same name; two abandoned ranches six leagues southeast of the presidio, one belonging to the San Ignacio Mission[52] and the other to Doña Sabina; the Arituava and Santa Rosa ranches belonging to the residents of Santa Ana village that had the largest population of Spaniards before the 1751 uprising and is now reduced to only a few; the San Lorenzo settlement four to five leagues northeast of Santa Ana which was abandoned in 1756 when the Seris and Pimas killed thirty-eight persons and burned down the pueblo; a small ranch-hamlet five leagues northwest of San Lorenzo called El Tupo[53] of which nothing remains but the name. The same is true of Rancho de la Navidad southwest of Santa Ana. It was destroyed by Apaches in 1730, and fourteen Christians were murdered.

---

[49] This is Cerro de San Antonio de Padua.

[50] 31 degrees, 10 minutes latitude by 262 degrees, 4 minutes longitude.

[51] A Spaniard born in Culiacán.

[52] San Ignacio de Caburica Mission.

[53] El Tupo was the site of the murder of ninety-eight Pimas by the soldiers of Lieutenant Antonio de Solís in June, 1695. The soldiers were trying to chastise the killers of Father Francisco Javier Saéta, S.J.

The pueblo of La Soledad and an adjacent ranch were destroyed in 1757 by an invasion of Apaches and Seris combined. Before that the same doom befell the farms of Sásava and one between San Ignacio and Cucurpe. Eastward there are no more inhabited places except the small town of Dolores and the real of Saracachi. The residents of Saracachi are few, so few that they do not feel they have sufficient numbers to dig up the great riches that, according to some, are contained in their mines. There is another deserted ranch north of Cucurpe and two others between Dolores and Remedios. The small settlement of San Javier, still occupied, lies to the south between Cucurpe and Toape.

We find the reales of Motepore[54] and Sonora[55] are still inhabited, as is the hacienda[56] of the late Bachelor Soto, but with no mines in operation. There is also the small real of San Joseph near Opodepe.

The following ranches are uninhabited because of the Apache and Seri incursions: Meresichi,[57] La Casita between Nacameri and Ures, another between Nacameri and Aconchi, and La Huerta north of Antúnez.

And the following reales have been abandoned because of the Seri enemy and his atrocities: Antúnez, Bacoachito, Gavilán, and San Cosme. There was either a farm or an estancia between Gavilán and San Cosme that was also abandoned. And the estancias of Alameda and Cornelio have been vacated as well as the Ybarburo ranch farther west near the Gulf of California. Moreover, the pearl placer of Tepoca to the north has been abandoned.

Nothing more remains inhabited except the settlements near and under the protection of the San Miguel de Horcasitas presidio such as the inoperative real of San José de Gracia, the ranch of Bachelor Don Francisco Javier Noriega, the hacienda of Pitic which was the property of the late governor, Don Agustín de Vildósola, a small community at

---

[54] Near Banámichi.

[55] Between Hüépac and Aconchi.

[56] The word hacienda may be applied not only to an agricultural establishment but also to a refining and assaying plant.

[57] Between San Joseph and Toape.

Cerro Pelón, another at Los Angeles, and the quite well populated but extremely poor community of San Miguel, contiguous to the presidio. This last community started calling itself villa at the time the Antúnez bonanza occurred, but I was not aware that it had been granted such a title. Therefore, I doubt it was entitled to that rank.

We have given the data pertaining to the founding of the San Miguel de Horcasitas presidio, 30 degrees latitude by 263 degrees, 30 minutes longitude, in chapter vi, section three. Now we close by stating that it is the residence of the governor[58] who is also the commander of the fort.

Out of respect and consideration for the well-being of the province, I prefer to say nothing about the erection of the five presidios.

To summarize briefly, on April 13, 1764,[59] there were in the province of Sonora:

Mining sites, Spanish settlements, and five presidios inhabited		22
Depopulated mining sites	48	
Inhabited estancias and ranches		2
Depopulated estancias and ranches	126	
Totals: Depopulated places	174	
Inhabited places		24

These figures do not include Santa Barbara, San Luis, Buenavista, or the five depopulated mining sites in the province of Ostimuri.

I beg the benevolent reader to forgive the disarray of the last two sections of this chapter. I confess that I thought they needed little discussion, so the subject was assembled hastily and left to the last. I promise that the section that follows will be better arranged.

---

[58] Col Juan Claudio Pineda was governor of Sonora from 1763 to 1770.

[59] The dates given in several places in the text seem inconsistent. As stated in the preface, Father Visitor Ignacio Lizassoian left Sonora on September 23, 1762, and Don José Tienda de Cuervo, governor of Sonora, left there on December 9, 1762. Both carried a copy of this essay. Then dates given after this time must have been the work of a copyist or copyists who updated the work.

SECTION THREE

Curacies: Their Vast Size and Places of Worship

Although the province of Sonora[60] is rather large and complex with many reales de minas, towns and ranches peopled by Spaniards and gente de razón, there are only three curacies. The first is San Juan Bautista which was abandoned May 3, 1751, as stated in chapter ix, section one, and while in a physical sense its church still remains, its minister[61] resides at San Miguel de Horcasitas where services are conducted in the presidio's chapel. The church edifice at San Miguel de Horcasitas was begun in 1753 by Governor Don Pablo de Arce y Arroyo during the boom days of the Antúnez gold mine. Today the edifice remains roofless and its adobe walls subjected to ruin by the rains. Because of the decadence of the Antúnez real, there is little hope the building will be completed unless a rich mine is discovered in that region soon. Its residents are extremely poor and support themselves solely by working their fertile land. But they have no outlet for their produce. They have plenty of food, but they go almost naked.

Another curacy is located at Nacozari[62] with a well equipped church of suitable capacity, but because of the meager population of the real of Nacozari and for security reasons, its father, Curate Don Joaquín Félix Díaz, resides at the presidio of Fronteras where he has better facilities for escort when he visits the ministries under his charge. Services are conducted in the fort's chapel, newly erected in 1763.

The areas of both these curacies are so large that the two priests, having no assistants, find it extremely difficult to attend them. To visit the places of their respective jurisdictions, each priest must travel more than two hundred leagues with imminent risk of being attacked by Apaches or Seris.

---

[60] In a religious sense the region was administered by three diocesan priests or curates, each holding the degree of Bachelor of Theology.

[61] In 1754 the Bachelor of Theology Gabriel Arenívar resigned the curacy of San Miguel de Horcasitas and the priest Francisco Javier Noriega filled the vacancy until the arrival of Miguel Arenívar.

[62] Nuestra Señora del Rosario de Nacozari.

The third curacy, San Francisco de Asís, is no smaller than the others, for it covers not only a part of Ostimuri Province but a good portion of Sonora as well, comprising the area from the right bank of the Yaqui River on the south and east to San Miguel de Horcasitas on the north, excluding Ures, Mátape, and Batuc. The residence of the curate, formerly in San Miguel,[63] is now in the real of Río Chico[64] in the province of Ostimuri. And because there are only three diocesan priests in Sonora, the Jesuit missionaries, without neglecting their own districts, help them as much as they can by imparting the faith, performing all religious functions and turning over all tithes collected to the curate. Because I am bound to tell the truth, I must say that the Jesuits ministering in this section do it all except in the place and its immediate vicinity where the curate Florencio de Alarcón, Bachelor of Theology, resides.[65] He does visit the closer churches occasionally, but as for the more distant parishes, he merely sends someone to gather the dues accrued through the labors of others.

Regardless of the size of these curacies, when the province was booming, not beset by enemies, all its pueblos inhabited and its mines worked with zeal and very productive, even then the province was not a large source of income for the church.

Father Juan José de Grijalva, Bachelor of Theology, informed me that the curacy he had administered for thirty years, the San Juan Bautista, had an estimated annual tithe income of two to three thousand pesos a year beyond his 2,000 pesos yearly salary. Yet he was only netting 1,000 pesos a year. To live with some degree of comfort he had to pledge the tithes to purchase a ranch.[66]

If the San Juan Bautista Curacy, supposedly the best in Sonora, was in such shape, it seems to me that the reason for its meager income was due to the charity of this venerable curate emeritus who condoned all dues to the poor, took livestock from others in payment,

---

63 This is San Miguel Arcángel, described in note 14, chapter ix, section one.

64 San Francisco de Asís de Río Chico.

65 Río Chico.

66 He purchased the Santa Barbara ranch.

and gave nearly all the revenues to his assistants in the parishes they attend. He passed away—*morte justorum*[67]—in January, 1763, and was buried in Our Lady of the Rosary Chapel[68] in the Oposura church.

The Nacozari Curacy could be as productive as the San Juan Bautista, perhaps even more so by as much as 300 pesos a year, because the Tubac presidio has been added to it. However, because the soldiers are not paid in coin but in goods at prices set by government regulations, this possible source of income is questionable.

These curacies are under the diocese of Durango. When a vacancy occurs, its bishop submits a list of three names of persons the bishop feels are competent to serve as curate in that curacy. The vicar selects one from the list whom he deems best suited for the post. However, since the curate of Nacozari, Don Joaquín Rodríguez Rey, was murdered by Apaches in 1755[69] despite the military escort that accompanied him, there are few diocesan priests willing to come to these regions. At present Joaquín Félix Díaz, vicar and ecclesiastic arbiter, is serving temporarily as curate. However, the curates of San Miguel de Horcasitas and Río Chico acquire their positions only after surviving competition and receive prebends which go with the post. The first was obtained by minister Miguel de Arenívar and the second by curate Florencio de Alarcón.

[67] "The death of the just."

[68] He is buried at the foot of the altar.

[69] Actually curate Rodríguez Rey was killed April 16, 1754.

X

How to Punish the Enemy and Prevent the Ruin of Sonora

I do not doubt that the enemies who are destroying and annihilating this province are a punishment from God and a scourge from His merciful hand, for such are the teachings in innumerable instances in the Sacred Scriptures as well as in ecclesiastical and secular histories. Consequently, the first and principal remedy is to appeal to Him with true penitence and fervent prayers. However, I am of the opinion that in addition we should employ the means which prudence, experience, and military art dictate. We have five presidios and many Spaniards and loyal Indian allies. Therefore, we should not be content with the first course only and expect the scourge to be lifted through miracles. That would be tempting God because His Divine Majesty wishes that effect should follow cause in the ordinary course of events. Thus, our obligation should be to pray to God and use our hands as the magnificent heroes, our ancestors, did when they undertook to throw off the Moorish yoke and conquer the vast empires of both Indies which, for the good of millions of souls, our great sovereign Charles III has under his rule. May God save him and increase his dominions even unto the confines of this New World. And may He lavish on his head laurel wreaths for the glory and triumph of the Holy Catholic faith. For in defense of this faith, Charles III has used his victorious armies with vigor so worthy of his Catholic heart.

Coming now to the subject of this section, I shall speak first of the Seris. It seems to me after what has been stated in chapter iv, section three, and chapter ix, sections one and two, the only remedy is to remove the Seris from our midst so completely that not a single one remains in this section of the country. They are so blood-thirsty that so long as the seed remains, the evil cannot be rooted out. And if they are to be deported, let it be to a distant land separated from this realm by a wide sea, wider than the Gulf of California isolated in all directions, for if they are left on the continent, they are sure to come back. They have been trained from childhood to remember and describe places, not by the right or left hand or in relation to other places, but by the direction of the winds. Take an Indian into any depths blindfolded, be it mines, dungeons, or intricate labyrinths, and turn him around a thousand times, he will still be able to tell toward what wind or direction he is facing as if he were a living compass. Thus, he will know how to set out and take the direction toward his country so long as there is no large sea in between. But he will undertake to cross a short stretch of water on a raft. The making and handling of rafts is an art in which the Seri is remarkably dexterous.

The same may be said of their confederates, the Pimas, for there is as little hope of converting them to the faith as there is of converting the Seris. For the past eleven years they have returned to their former wild and barbarous life and committed the same and even worse crimes than the Seris. Because they are delinquents, apostates, incorrigible, and obstinately harmful to the Crown and the public, they should be deported or made to serve as oarsmen in the Royal galleys. If this were done, they should have no grievance, and the expense incurred for their transportation would be more than offset by the benefit to the rich mining settlements, pearl fisheries, haciendas, and estancias which are now abandoned because of their hostilities. The land offers many advantages for the breeding of livestock, but because of the Pima menace, livestock, especially horses, is scarce in this province. Now they must be brought from distant places.

With regard to controlling and humbling the arrogance of the Apache, the boldest enemy of Sonora, if the Crown does not provide greater numbers of soldiers, I am of the opinion that the few we have will do more harm than good on their occasional expeditions. All they accomplish in such forays is to kill a few aged Apaches, some youthful good-for-nothings, and bring back women and children as captives. And the soldiers are able to do this only occasionally, not always. Soon after such a raid, the Apaches take triple revenge, overrunning the province, committing murders and other atrocities, and taking a few unfortunate prisoners. We are at a disadvantage, because in order to carry out our excursions it is necessary to call out the Indian auxiliaries who make several journeys carrying provisions and searching for the hideouts of the enemy who is constantly on the move. Where there is no house to ransack nor any livestock to confiscate, but only an occasional deerskin to take, there is little hope of defraying the cost of the expedition. On the other hand, the Apaches go to settlements that are quite familiar to them and travel on roads they know well. They are able to prepare their ambushes and carry out their cruelties without fear, and they know they will find livestock and crops for their sustenance. So, unless we change our tactics, the enemy, having the advantage, will continue his raids indefinitely.

Knowing Sonora and taking into consideration all aspects of the problem, I am of the opinion, as are the more responsible and experienced citizens, that instead of expeditions into enemy territory, the borders along the frontier from one presidio to another should be patrolled, and when enemy tracks are found, they must be followed. The villages in the direction in which the enemy is moving must be alerted so that they can be prepared to offer resistance, or perhaps they will congregate at a given point a short distance from the pueblo where they will have provisions for the few days they will be out. This plan, though not acceptable to the commanders of the presidios, would be looked upon favorably by the residents and their Indian allies and would prevent the head of a patrol from ordering a return to the fort on the pretext that "it is not convenient" to resist. This has happened with disservice to the Crown, harm to the homeland, and deflation to the spirit of the inhabitants of this unhappy province. Besides leaving the auxiliaries utterly disgusted at seeing themselves abandoned, it leaves the enemy more arrogant than before.

This suggested plan is supported by the fact that the enemy makes short marches and travels slowly until they find a favorable opening to commit a few killings. They take some captives and livestock and then, in fear of the chase, hurry away. This could be prevented if the residents were alerted and their auxiliaries offered resistance at the moment the enemy tried to enter. Therefore, I believe that if this plan is followed, within one year the enemy would have no desire to come back and would set about finding another way to get along in his own territory. Then, Sonora being somewhat recovered, some thought could be given to converting the Apaches to Christianity or subjugating them by force.

May God our Lord enlighten the minds of those who can remedy so many evils so that they may take the necessary measures to maintain the faithful Indians within the fold. And may God our Lord free those faithful Indians from the attacks of so cruel an enemy, and in the enjoyment of peace, open the gates of the Catholic faith to the vast country of heathens for the greater glory of God and the everlasting memory and inestimable increase of the dominions of our Catholic Monarch.

Bibliography and References

Academia Mexicana de Historia. *Memorias.* Quarterly publication. 30 vols. México, D.F., 1932–1971.

Acosta, Joseph de, S.J. *Historia natural y moral de las indias 1590.* México, D.F., 1962.

Alcocer, Gabriel V. "Catálogo de las frutas comestibles." In *Anales del Museo Nacional de México*. Second epoch, vol. **II**. México, D.F., 1905.

Alegre, Francisco J., S.J. *Historia de la Compañía de Jesús en Nueva España.* Burrus-Zubillaga version. 4 vols. Rome, 1956–1960.

Almada, Francisco R. *Chínipas —Apuntes historicos.* Chihuahua, 1937.

———. *Diccionario de historia, geografía y biografía sonorenses.* Chihuahua, 1952.

Archivo general de la Nación [AGN]. *Boletín.* Quarterly publication. 1st series, 30 vols. 1930–1959; 2nd series, 12 vols. to 1971. México, D.F.

Balthasar, Juan Antonio. "Información destos padres misioneros desta provincia de Sonora, como se hallan al acabar esta visita de el año 1744." Manuscript in the Beinecke Rare Book and Manuscript Library (Yale University, New Haven).

Bancroft, Hubert Howe. *History of Arizona and New Mexico.* In *The Works of Hubert Howe Bancroft* **XVII**. 39 vols. San Francisco, 1889.

———. *Native Races.* In *The Works of Hubert Howe Bancroft* **I–V**. 39 vols. San Francisco, 1880–86.

———. *North Mexican States.* In *The Works of Hubert Howe Bancroft* **XV–XVI**. 39 vols. San Francisco, 1884–1889.

Bannon, John F. *The Mission Frontier in Sonora, 1620–1687.* New York, 1955.

Barajas-Casso-López, Esperanza. *Los animales en la medicina popular mexicana.* México, D.F., 1951.

Barlow, R. H. "La Relacion de Sahuaripa de 1778." *Memorias de la Academia Mexicana de la historia* **VI**, no. 1 (1947):60–89.

Beals, Ralph L. *Comparative Ethnology of Northern Mexico Before 1750.* Ibero-Americana series, no. 2. Berkeley, 1932.

Bennett, Wendell C. and Robert M. Zingg. *The Tarahumara. An Indian Tribe of Northern Mexico.* Chicago, 1955.

Benson, Lyman and Robert A. Darrow. *A Manual of Southwestern Desert Trees and Shrubs.* Tucson, 1944.

Boletín del Archivo General de la Nación (AGN). 1st series, 30 vols. 1930–1959; 2nd series, 12 vols to 1971. México, D.F.

Bolton, Herbert E. *Anza's California Expeditions* **II** and **IV**. 5 vols. Berkeley, 1930.

———. *Kino's Historical Memoir of Pimería Alta*. Berkeley, 1948.

———. *Padre on Horseback*. Chicago, 1963.

———. *Rim of Christendom*. New York, 1936.

Bravo, Helia. *Las cactáceas de México*. México, D.F., 1937.

Burrus, Ernest J., S.J. *Historia de México del P. Andrés Cavo*. México, D.F., 1949.

———. *Kino and the Cartography of Northwestern New Spain*. Tucson, 1965.

———. *La obra cartográfica de la provincia Mexicana de la Compañía de Jesús*. 2 vols. Madrid, 1967.

———. *Vida del P. Francisco J. Saéta*. México, D.F., 1961.

Cabrera, Luis G. *Plantas curativas de México*. 2nd ed. México, D.F., 1943.

Calderón de la Barca. *Life in Mexico—during a residence of two years in that country*. London, 1843.

Calvo-Berber, Laureano. *Nociones de historia de Sonora*. México, D.F., 1958.

Campo, Rafaél Martín del. "Aves en la historia antigua de México." *Boletín de la Sociedad de Geografía y Estadística* **LXXIII**. México, D.F., 1952.

Cañas, Cristóbal de, S.J. "Estado y descripción de la provincia de Sonora." In *Documentos para la historia de México* **XVI**, pp. 617–37.

Cantú Treviño, Sara. *La vega de Metztitlán*. State of Hidalgo. México, D.F., 1953.

Cárdenas y Cano, Gabriel (pen name of Andrés González de Barcia). *Ensayo cronológico para la historia general de la Florida*. Madrid, 1723.

Cartas anuas (litterae annuae). Letters to and from Jesuit headquarters in Rome. Mexican Province.

Catálogo de los sujetos de la Compañía de Jesús que formaban la provincia de México el día del arresto, 25 de junio de 1767. Begun by Father Rafael Zelis, S.J., and completed by Father Pedro Márquez, 1786. México, D.F., 1871.

Catalogues of the Jesuit members of the Order in the Mexican Province, issued yearly from the Mexico City office of the Provincial.

Cavo, Andrés. *Los tres siglos de México durante el gobierno Español hasta la entrada del Ejército Trigarante*. Notes and supplement by Carlos María Bustamante. México, D.F., 1852.

Clark, Phil. *A Guide to Mexican Flora*. México, D.F., 1964.

Clavijero, Francisco Javier, S.J. *Historia antigua de México y su conquista, sacada de los mejores historiadores españoles, y de los manuscritos y pinturas antiguas de los indios: dividida en diez libros: adornada con mapas y estampas, e ilustrada con disertaciones sobre la tierra, los animales y los habitantes de México*. Traducción Mora. 2 vols. México, D.F., 1844.

———. *Historia de la antigua o Baja California*. Traducción García de San Vicente, México, D.F., 1852.

Colección de documentos inéditos relativos al descubrimiento, conquista y colonización de las antiguas posesiones Españolas en América y Oceanía. Joaquín F.

Pacheco, Francisco Cárdenas, y Luis Torres de Mendoza, editores. 1st series, 42 volumes, 1864–1884; 2nd series, 25 volumes. Madrid, 1885–1900.

"Convite Evangélico y compasión y socorro de la viña del Señor, destrozada y conculcada con el alzamiento de la Pimería Alta desde el 21 de noviembre del año 1751 y sus lastimosos progresos en la siguiente década hasta el año de 1760." Anonymous, unpublished manuscript at the University of California at Los Angeles. Indexed as "An account of the uprising against the Jesuit missions in California from 1751–1766."

Cozzens, Samuel Woodworth. *The Ancient Cibola. The Marvellous Country or Three Years in Arizona and New Mexico.* Lee and Shepard, Boston, 1891.

Curtin, L. S. M. *Healing Herbs of the Upper Río Grande.* Santa Fe, 1947.

Dávila, Francisco T. *Sonora histórico y descriptivo.* Nogales, Arizona, 1894.

Dávila Garibí, J. I. *Observaciones sobre la lengua Opata o Tegüima.* México, D.F., 1950.

Decorme, Gerard, S.J. *La obra de los Jesuitas Mexicanos.* 2 vols. México, D.F., 1941.

DiPeso, Charles C. "The Seri Indians as Described by Adamo Gilg, S.J., in 1692." Written with Daniel S. Matson. *Arizona and the West* **VII**, no. 1 (spring 1965):33–56.

———. *The Sobaipuri Indians of the Upper San Pedro River Valley, Southeastern Arizona.* Dragoon, Arizona, 1953.

Documentos Instituto Médico Nacional. Secretaría de Fomento. México, D.F., 1888.

Documentos para la historia de México. 20 vols. Published by Manuel Orozco y Berra in four series. México, D.F., 1856. Vol. **16** includes first Spanish version of the *Rudo Ensayo.*

Donohue, J. A., S.J. *After Kino. Jesuit Missions in Northwestern New Spain 1711–67.* Rome, 1969.

Dunne, Peter Masten, S.J. *Balthazar, Padre Visitador to the Sonora Frontier, 1744–1745.* Tucson, 1957.

———. *Black Robes in Lower California.* Berkeley, 1952.

———. "Capitán Anza and the Case of Father Campos." *Mid-America* **23**, I (1941):45–60. Chicago.

———. Trans. of Jacobo Sedelmayr's *Missionary, Frontiersman, Explorer in Arizona and Sonora 1744–1751.* Tucson, 1955.

———. *Pioneer Jesuits in Northern Mexico.* Berkeley, 1944.

Escudero, José Agustín. *Noticias estadísticas de Sonora y Sinaloa.* México, D.F., 1849.

Ewing, Charles R. "The Pima Uprising of 1751." In *Greater America.* Berkeley, 1945.

Font's Complete Diary. Trans. by Herbert E. Bolton in *Anza's California Expeditions* **IV**. Berkeley, 1930.

Gándara, Guillermo. "Origen de las calabazas de México." In *Memorias y Revista* **53** (1932) of the Academia Nacional de Ciencias de México (founded in 1884; formerly Academia "Antonio Alzate").

González de Barcia, Andrés [pen name of Gabriel Cárdenas y Cano]. *Ensayo cronológico para la historia general de la Florida.* Madrid, 1723.

González Obregón, Luis. *México Viejo. Noticias históricas, tradiciones y leyendas.* México, D.F., 1900.

Granillo, Francisco Pérez. "Descripción particular de las naciones, pueblos, ríos, valles y tierras y minas de la provincia de Sonora." In *Documentos para la historia de México,* cuarta serie, Tomo **I,** pp. 391–402.

Guiteras, Eusebio. Trans. of Nentvig's *Rudo Ensayo.* American Catholic Historical Society, Philadelphia, 1894; republished by Arizona Silhouettes, Tucson, 1951.

Gulick, Howard E. *Nayarit. A Guide Book.* Glendale, 1965.

Gulick, Howard E. and Peter Gerhard. *Lower California Guide Book.* Glendale, 1962.

Gumilla, Joseph, S.J. *El Orinoco ilustrado, historia natural, civil y geográfica de este gran río y de sus caudalosas vertientes; gobierno, usos y costumbres de los indios sus habitadores, con nuevas y útiles noticias de animales, árboles, frutos, aceites, resinas, yerbas y raíces medicinales, y sobre todo, se hallarán conversiones muy singulares a nuestra santa fe y casos de mucha edificación.* Madrid, 1741.

Hastings, J. R. "People of Reason and Others." *Arizona and the West* **III** (winter 1965):321–40.

Hernández, Fortunato. *Las razas indígenas de Sonora.* México, D.F., 1902.

Hernández, Francisco. *Historia de las plantas de Nueva España.* 3 vols. México, D.F., 1946.

Hernández de Oviedo, Gonzalo. *De la natural historia de las Indias.* Madrid, 1942.

Hernández Rodríguez, Rosaura. "Epidemias y calamidades en el México prehispánico." In *Anuario de Historia,* publication of the Mexican University, 1962.

Hernández Sánchez-Barba, Mario. *Ultima expansión Española en América.* Madrid, 1957.

Hrdlička, Aleš. "Notes on the Indians of Sonora, Mexico." *The American Anthropologist* **VI,** no. 1 (January–March 1901):51–89.

Humboldt, Alexander. *Ensayo político sobre el reino de la Nueva España.* México, D.F., 1966.

Johnson, Jean B. *The Opata. An Inland Tribe of Sonora.* Albuquerque, 1950.

Kennard, William C. and Harold F. Winters. *Some Fruits and Nuts for the Tropics.* Washington, D.C., 1960.

Kessell, John L. "A Personal Note from Tumacacori, 1825." *Journal of Arizona History* **VI,** no. 3 (autumn 1965):147–51.

________. *Mission of Sorrows. Jesuit Guevavi and the Pimas 1691–1767.* Tucson, 1970.

________. "The Puzzling Presidio." *New Mexico Historical Review* **XLI,** no. 1 (January 1966):21–46.

Kino, Eusebio Francisco, S.J. *Favores Celestiales.* Cf. Kino's *Las Misiones de Sonora y Arizona.*

________. *Las Misiones de Sonora y Arizona.* Version Francisco Fernández del Castillo. Vol. **VIII** of AGN publications. México, D.F., 1913–22.

———. *Vida del P. Francisco J. Saéta.* Annotated by E. J. Burrus, S.J. México, D.F., 1961.

Landis, Sam W. *A Hunter's Guide to Mexico–Minutiae Mexicana.* México, D.F., 1965.

Lizassoian, Ignacio. "Informe sobre las provincias de Sonora y Nueva Vizcaya al Exmo. Sr. Virrey Marqués de Cruillas: 14 de diciembre 1762." In *Documentos para la historia.* 3ra serie, tercera parte, pp. 683–702. México, D.F., 1856.

Lockwood, F. C. *With Padre Kino on the Trail.* Tucson, 1934.

López de Gómara, Francisco. *Historia general de las Indias.* Madrid, 1941.

López, Gregorio. *Tesoro de medicinas para diversas enfermedades, con notas de los doctores Mathías de Salzedo Mariaca y Joseph Díaz Brizuela.* México, D.F., 1673.

Lumholtz, Carl. *Unknown Mexico.* 2 vols. Glorieta, New Mexico. 1973.

Mange, Juan Mateo. *Luz de tierra incógnita en la América septentrional y diario de las exploraciones en Sonora.* México, D.F., 1926.

Martínez, Maximino. *Las plantas medicinales de México.* México, D.F., 1969.

Mateu, Jaime, S.J. "Colección de cartas de varios Jesuitas en el noroeste de Nueva España." In *El destierro.* 1745. 2 vols. Extant in the Fondo Jesuítico, Biblioteca Nazionale, Rome.

Memorias Academia Mexicana de la Historia. Quarterly publication, 30 vols. México, D.F., 1932–1971.

Mendizabal, Miguel O. *La evolución del noroeste de México.* México, D.F., 1930.

Molina, Flavio. *Nombres indígenas de Sonora.* Hermosillo, Sonora, México, 1972.

Morfi, Fray Juan Agustín de. *Diario y Derrotero 1777–1781.* Monterrey, Mexico, 1967.

Navarro García, Luis. *Don José de Gálvez y la comandancia general de las provincias internas del norte de Nueva España.* Sevilla, 1964.

———. *La sublevación Yaqui de 1740.* Sevilla, 1966.

———. *Sonora y Sinaloa en el siglo XVII.* Sevilla, 1967.

Nentvig, Juan, S.J. Letters: To Father José Hidalgo, S.J., October 3, 1766, located in the Temporalidades section, legajo 17–24, Archivo Histórico de Hacienda, Mexico City.

To Don Joaquín de Montserrat, the Marquis de Cruillas, July 15, 1764, located in the Archivo General de la Nación, Mexico City, Provincias internas section, vol. 86, folios 332–3.

To provincial Francisco Zeballos, S.J., two letters, July 16, 1764, and February 14, 1765, *ibid.* The latter appears in *Mid-Winter* **24**, new series, no. 2, 87–9.

To visitor general José Utrera, S.J., December 3, 1754, located in the Archivo Franciscano, Biblioteca Nacional, caja 33–692, Mexico City, and published in *Documentos para la historia de México* **I**, second series, pp. 195–204.

———. *Descripción geográfica, natural y curiosa de la provincia de Sonora por un amigo de el servicio de Dios y de el Rey Nuestro Señor.* Edition prepared by Germán Viveros. México, D.F., 1971.

Nentvig, Juan, S.J. *(Continued)*

———. *Rudo Ensayo.* Buckingham Smith version. St Augustine, 1863.

———. *Rudo Ensayo.* Eusebio Guiteras translation. Philadelphia, 1894; Tucson, 1951.

———. *Rudo Ensayo.* Vol. **393.** Manuscript in the Archivo general de la Nación, (AGN). México, D.F., 1764.

Noticias varias de Nueva Galicia, intendencia de Guadalajara. Published by the state of Jalisco, a series of articles that first appeared in the newspaper *El Estado de Jalisco.* Guadalajara, México, 1878.

Obregón, Balthasar. *Historia de los descubrimientos antiguos y modernos de Nueva España, 1584.* México, D.F., 1924.

Ocaranza, Fernando. *Crónicas y relaciones del occidente de México.* 2 vols. México, D.F., 1939.

———. *Parva crónica de la Sierra Madre y las Pimerías.* México, D.F., 1942.

Och, Joseph, S.J. *Missionary in Sonora.* Translation by T. F. Treutlein. San Francisco, 1965.

Orozco y Berra, Manuel, *Documentos para la historia de México,* 20 vols. in 4 series. Vol. 1, fourth series, México, D. F., 1856.

Ortega, José, S.J. *Apostólicos afanes. Historia del Nayarit, Sonora, Sinaloa y ambas Californias.* México, D.F., 1887.

Oviedo, Gonzalo Fernández de. *De la natural historia de las indias.* Annotated by Enrique Alvarez López. 2 vols. Madrid, 1942.

Peña, Salvador Ignacio de la, S.J. In "Convite evangélico," unpublished MS, University of California, Los Angeles.

Pérez Hernández, José M. *Geografía del estado de Sonora.* México, D.F., 1872.

Pérez Ribas, Andrés, S.J. *Historia de los triunfos de nuestra Santa Fe entre las gentes mas bárbaras y fieras del nuevo Orbe.* 3 vols. Madrid, 1645; México, D.F., 1944.

Pesman, M. Walter. *Flora mexicana.* Flagstaff, 1962.

Pfefferkorn, Ignaz, S.J. *Description of Sonora.* Treutlein's translation. Albuquerque, 1949.

Pimentel, Francisco Antonio. "Diario de lo acaecido y practicado en la entrada que se hizo a la Isla de Tiburón en 1750." *Boletín del Archivo General de la Nación.* First series, vol. **XVII**, no. 4. México, D.F., 1946.

Pólize, Horacio, S.J. "Relación de la pimería que remite el Padre Visitador." In *Documentos para la historia de México.* Tercera serie, vol. **XVI**. México, D.F., 1857.

Polzer, Charles William, S.J. *The Evolution of the Jesuit Mission System in Northwestern New Spain, 1600–1767.* Doctoral dissertation, University of Arizona, 1972.

Ponce de León, José M. "Datos geográficos y estadísticos de Chihuahua." In *Boletín de la Sociedad Mexicana de Geografía y Estadística* **I-II**. México, D.F., 1906–1907.

Pradeau, Alberto F. "Description of Sonora," *Mid-America* **24** new series, no. 2 (April 1953):81–90.

———. *Expulsión de los Jesuitas de las provincias de Sonora, Ostimuri y Sinaloa.* Mexico, D.F., 1959.

Ridgway, Robert and Herbert Friedmann. *Birds of North and Middle America.* Washington, D.C., 1941.

Rivera, Pedro de. *Diario y derrotero de lo caminado, visto y observado en la visita que hizo a los presidios de la Nueva España septentrional.* México, D.F., 1946.

Roca, Paul M. *Paths of the Padres Through Sonora.* Tucson, 1967.

Rodríguez Gallardo, José R. *"Informe sobre Sonora."* Vol. **29**. Manuscript in AGN, Provincias Internas Section.

Rodríguez, Luis A. *La ciencia médica de los Aztecas.* México, D.F., 1944.

Román y Zamora, Fr. Jerónimo. *Repúblicas de Indias, idolatrías y gobierno.* Madrid, 1897.

Romo de Vivar, José, Pedro García de Almazán, Pedro de Peralta y Francisco Mendoza. "Informe sobre Sonora." February 6, 1693. In *Historical Documents of Adolph and Fanny Bandellier.* Vol. **II**:290–7. 3 vols. Washington, D.C., 1923–1927.

Roxas, Carlos de. "Bosquejo histórico de la misión de Nuestra Señora de la Asunsión de Arizpe, 28 de julio, 1744." Manuscript in Bancroft Library, University of California, Berkeley.

———. "Visita de la provincia de Sonora, año de 1748." Folder 278, document 17. Manuscript in Archivo general de la Nación (AGN). México, D.F.

Sahagún, Fr. Bernardino. *Historia general de las cosas de Nueva España.* 3 vols. México, D.F., 1946.

Santamaría, Francisco J. *Diccionario de Americanismos.* 3 vols. México, D.F., 1942.

———. *Diccionario de Mejicanismos.* México, D.F., 1959.

Sauer, Carl. *Aboriginal Population of Northwestern Mexico.* Ibero-Americana series, no. 10. Berkeley, 1935.

———. *Aboriginal Tribes and Languages in Northwestern Mexico.* Ibero-Americana series, no. 5. Berkeley, 1934.

Sedelmayr, Jacobo, S.J. *Missionary, Frontiersman, Explorer in Arizona and Sonora 1744–1751.* Translated and annotated by Peter Masten Dunne. Tucson, 1955.

Ségesser, Felipe. "The Relation of Philip Ségesser. The Pimas and Other Indians," T. E. Treutlein, translator, in *Mid-America* **27**,3 (July 1945):139–87.

Shreve, Forrest and Ira L. Wiggins. *Vegetation and Flora of the Sonoran Desert.* Palo Alto, 1964.

Simpson, Lesley Byrd. *Administration of the Indians in New Spain.* Berkeley, 1940.

———. *José Longinos Martínez—California in 1792.* San Marino, 1938.

Smith, Buckingham. Nentvig's *Rudo Ensayo.* St Augustine, 1863.

Sobarzo, Horacio. *Vocabulario Sonorense.* México, D.F., 1966.

Spicer, Edward H. *Cycles of Conquest.* Tucson, 1967.

Standley, Paul C. *Trees and Shrubs of Mexico.* Washington, D.C., 1920.

Tamarón y Romeral, Pedro. *Demostración del vastísimo obispado de Nueva Vizcaya.* México, D.F., 1937.

Thornberger, John J. and Frances Bonker. *The Fantastic Clan.* New York, 1932.

Torquemada, Fray Juan. *Monarquía Indiana, 1723.* 3 vols. México, D.F., 1943.

Trens, Manuel B. "Arte curativo de las enfermedades. Farmacia y Hechicería." *Boletín* AGN **XXIII**, no. 4 (1952):495–559.

———. *México de antaño.* México, D.F., 1957.

Treutlein, Theodore F. "Jesuit Missionaries in the Role of Physician." *Mid-America* **22**, no. 2 (April 1940):120–41.

———. "The Economic Regime of the Jesuit Missions in 18th Century Sonora." *Pacific Historical Review* **VIII** (September 1939):289–300.

———. Trans. of Och's *Missionary in Sonora.* San Francisco, 1965.

———. Trans. of Pfefferkorn's *Description of Sonora.* Albuquerque, 1949.

———. "Pfefferkorn's Description of Sonora." *Mid-America* **20**, no. 1 (October 1938):229–32.

Van Rossem, A. J. *A Distributional Survey of the Birds of Sonora, Mexico.* Baton Rouge, 1945.

Velarde, Luis, S.J. "A Description of the Site, Longitude and Latitude of the Nations of the Pimería, with its Northern Adjacents, Its California Gulf and Other Notices and Observations Made by the Reverend Father." *New Mexico Historical Review* **VI**, no. 2 (April 1931):111–57.

———. "Relación." Cf. supra Velarde's first entry.

Velasco, José Francisco. *Noticias estadísticas de Sonora.* México, D.F., 1850.

———. *Noticias estadísticas de Sonora.* In *Boletín de la Sociedad Mexicana de Geografía y Estadística* **VIII-XI.** México, D.F., 1860–1865.

Velásquez de la Cadena. *A New Pronouncing Dictionary of Spanish and English Languages.* 2 vols. New York, 1902.

Venegas, Miguel, S.J. *Noticia de la California y de sus conquistas temporal y espiritual hasta el tiempo presente.* 3 vols. 1st edition, Madrid, 1757; 2nd edition, México, D.F., 1944.

Villa, Eduardo W. *Compendio historia de Sonora.* México, D.F., 1937.

Villaseñor y Sánchez, Joseph Antonio de. *Teatro americano. Descripción general de los reynos y provincias de la Nueva España y sus jurisdicciones.* México, D.F., 1746.

Viveros, Germán. Edition of Nentvig's *Descripción geográfica.* AGN, México, D.F., 1971.

Ward, H. G. *Mexico in 1827.* 2 vols. Appendix, vol. **I**:559–91. London, 1828.

Wilson, Baronesa de. *México y sus gobernantes.* 2 vols. México, D.F., 1958.

Zambrano, Francisco, S.J. *Diccionario Bio-Bibliográfico de la Compañía de Jesús en México.* 16 vols. México, D.F., 1961–1977.

Zelis, Rafael, S.J., and Father Pedro Márquez. *Catálogo de los sujetos de la Compañía de Jesús que formaban la provincia de México el día del arresto, 25 de junio de 1767.* México, D.F., 1871.

Zim, Herbert S. and Alexander C. Martin. *Trees.* New York, 1956.

Zorita, Alonzo de. *Historia de la Nueva España.* Vol. **I** (the only one published), pp. 122–30. Madrid, 1909.

General Index

Index to Fauna, Flora, and Ailments

Nentvig's Map of Sonora and Areas North, 1762. Retouched by A. F. Pradeau. Reproduced by courtesy of the British Museum.

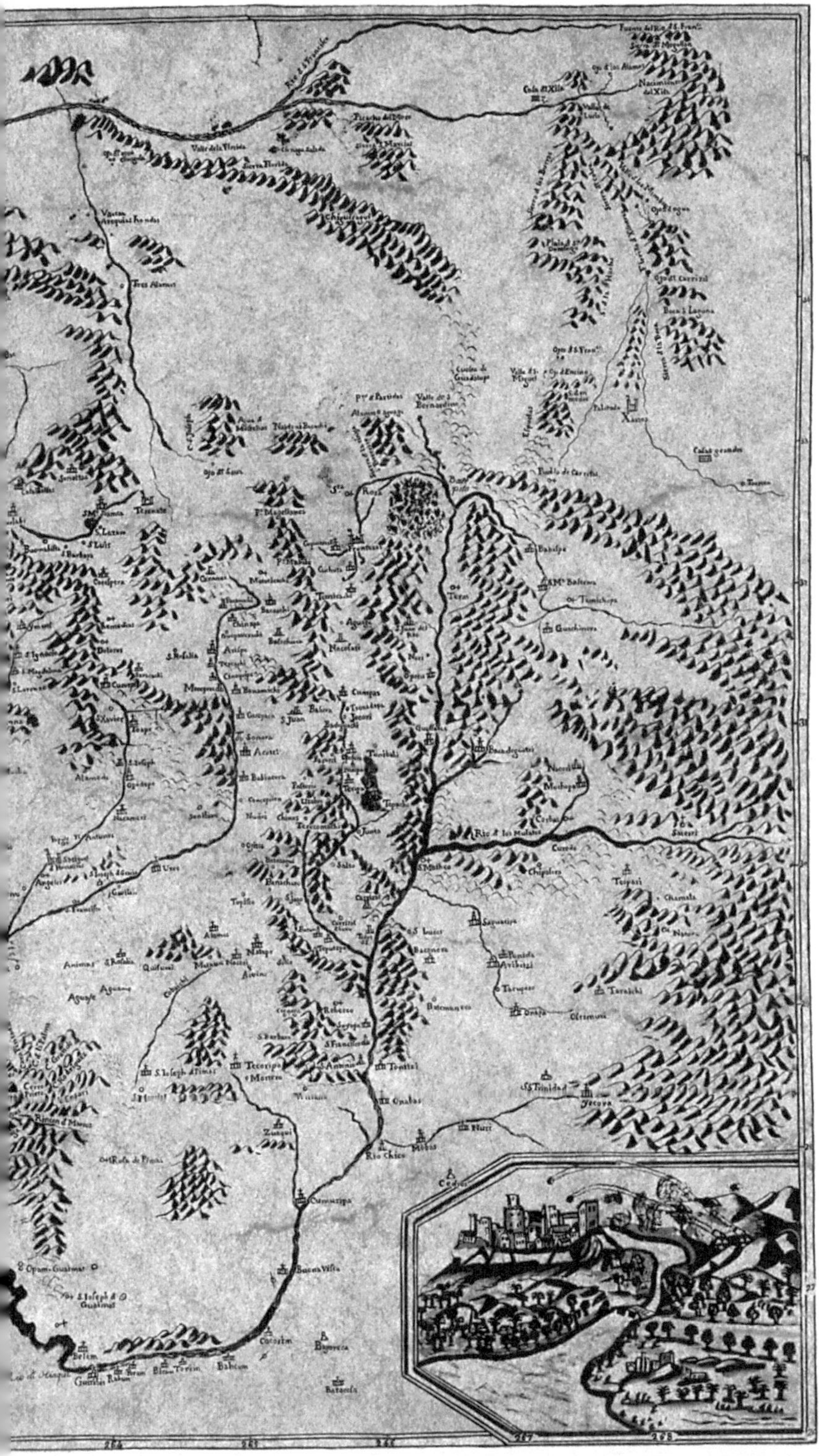
Tres Alamos
Rio Chico
Buena Vista
Casas grandes